TRANSLATION

OF SEVERAL

PRINCIPAL BOOKS, PASSAGES, AND TEXTS

OF

THE VEDS

TRANSLATION

OF SEVERAL

PRINCIPAL BOOKS, PASSAGES, AND TEXTS

OF

THE VEDS

AND OF

SOME CONTROVERSIAL WORKS

ON

BRAHMUNICAL THEOLOGY

RAJAH RAMMOHUN ROY

GYAN

Published by

GYAN

Gyan Publishing House
5, Ansari Road
Daryaganj, New Delhi-110002
Phone: 011-47034999, 9811692060
E-mail: books@gyanbooks.com

Distribution Network
gyanbooks.com
India, USA, Canada, UK, Australia, France

ISBN: 978-81-212-9120-0 (PB)
First Published, 1832

2nd Impression 2023

Printed at: Gyan Press, Delhi.

TRANSLATION OF SEVERAL PRINCIPAL BOOKS, PASSAGES, AND TEXTS OF THE VEDS

AUTHOR: RAJAH RAMMOHUN ROY

TRANSLATION

OF SEVERAL

PRINCIPAL BOOKS, PASSAGES, AND TEXTS

OF

THE VEDS.

TRANSLATION

OF SEVERAL

PRINCIPAL BOOKS, PASSAGES, AND TEXTS

OF

THE VEDS,

AND OF

SOME CONTROVERSIAL WORKS

ON

BRAHMUNICAL THEOLOGY.

BY

RAJAH RAMMOHUN ROY.

SECOND EDITION.

LONDON:
PARBURY, ALLEN, & CO.,
LEADENHALL STREET.

1832.

CONTENTS.

INTRODUCTION.

Several of my friends having expressed a wish to be possessed of copies of my Translation of the Veds, and Controversies with those Brahmuns who are advocates for idolatry, I have collected for republication such of those tracts as I could find, either among my own papers or those of my friends who happened to have brought them from India, and now offer them to the public in their original form.

I feel induced to set forth here, briefly, the substance of these writings, to facilitate the comprehension of their purport, as being foreign to the generality of European readers. The Veds (or properly speaking, the spiritual parts of them) uniformly declare, that man is prone by nature, or by habit, to reduce the object or objects of his veneration and worship (though admitted to be unknown) to tangible forms, ascribing to such objects attributes, supposed excellent according to his own notions; whence idolatry, gross or refined, takes its origin, and perverts the true course of intellect to vain fancies. These authorities, therefore, hold out precautions against framing a deity after human imagination, and recommend mankind to direct all researches towards the surrounding objects, viewed either collectively or individually, bearing in mind their regular, wise, and wonderful combinations and arrangements; since such researches cannot fail, they affirm, to lead an unbiassed mind to a notion of a Supreme Existence, who so sublimely designs and disposes of them, as is every where traced through the universe. The same Veds represent rites and external worship addressed to the planets and elementary objects, or personified abstract notions, as well as to deified heroes, as intended for persons of mean capacity; but enjoin spiritual devotion, as already described, benevolence, and self-control, as the only means of securing bliss.

RAMMOHUN ROY.

London, July 23, 1832.

P.S. In all the following Translations, except the Céna Upanishad, the mode of spelling Sanscrit words in English, adopted by Dr. J. B. Gilchrist, has been observed.

TRANSLATION

OF AN

ABRIDGMENT

OF

THE VEDANT,

OR

RESOLUTION OF ALL THE VEDS;

THE

MOST CELEBRATED AND REVERED WORK OF

Brahminical Theology;

ESTABLISHING THE UNITY OF THE SUPREME BEING; AND THAT

HE ALONE

IS THE OBJECT OF PROPITIATION AND WORSHIP.

CALCUTTA:
1816.

TO

THE BELIEVERS OF THE ONLY TRUE GOD.

THE greater part of Brahmins, as well as of other sects of Hindoos, are quite incapable of justifying that idolatry which they continue to practise. When questioned on the subject, in place of adducing reasonable arguments in support of their conduct, they conceive it fully sufficient to quote their ancestors as positive authorities! And some of them are become very ill-disposed towards me, because I have forsaken idolatry for the worship of the true and eternal God! In order, therefore, to vindicate my own faith and that of our early forefathers, I have been endeavouring, for some time past, to convince my countrymen of the true meaning of our sacred books; and to prove, that my aberration deserves not the opprobrium which some unreflecting persons have been so ready to throw upon me.

The whole body of the Hindoo Theology, Law, and Literature, is contained in the Veds, which are affirmed to be coeval with the creation! These works are extremely voluminous; and being written in the most elevated and metaphorical style, are, as may be well supposed, in many passages seemingly confused and contradictory. Upwards of two thousand years ago, the great Byas, reflecting on the perpetual difficulty arising from these sources, composed with great discrimination a complete and compendious abstract of the whole; and also reconciled those texts which appeared to stand at variance. This work he termed *The Vedant*, which, compounded of two Sungscrit words, signifies *The Resolution of all the Veds.* It has continued to be most highly revered by all the Hindoos; and in place of the more diffuse arguments of the Veds, is always referred to as equal authority. But from its being concealed within the dark curtain of the Sungscrit language, and the Brahmins permitting themselves alone to interpret, or even to touch any book of the kind, the Vedant, although perpetually quoted, is little known to the public: and the practice of few Hindoos indeed bears the least accordance with its precepts!

In pursuance of my vindication, I have to the best of my abilities translated this hitherto unknown work, as well as an abridgment thereof, into the Hindoostanee and Bengalee languages; and distributed them, free of cost, among my own countrymen, as widely as circumstances have possibly allowed. The present is an endeavour to render an abridgment of the same into English, by which I expect to prove to my European friends, that the superstitious practices which deform the Hindoo religion have nothing to do with the pure spirit of its dictates!

I have observed, that both in their writings and conversation, many Europeans feel a wish to palliate and soften the features of Hindoo idolatry; and are inclined to inculcate, that all objects of worship are considered by their votaries as emblematical representations of the

Supreme Divinity!—If this were indeed the case, I might perhaps be led into some examination of the subject: but the truth is, the Hindoos of the present day have no such views of the subject; but firmly believe in the real existence of innumerable gods and goddesses, who possess, in their own departments, full and independent power; and to propitiate them, and not the true God, are temples erected and ceremonies performed. There can be no doubt, however, and it is my whole design to prove, that every rite has its derivation from the allegorical adoration of the true Deity; but at the present day all this is forgotten, and among many it is even heresy to mention it!

I hope it will not be presumed that I intend to establish the preference of my faith over that of other men. The result of controversy on such a subject, however multiplied, must be ever unsatisfactory; for the reasoning faculty which leads men to certainty in things within its reach, produces no effect on questions beyond its comprehension. I do no more than assert, that, if correct reasoning, and the dictates of common sense, induce the belief of a wise, uncreated Being, who is the supporter and ruler of the boundless universe, we should also consider him the most powerful and supreme existence;—far surpassing our powers of comprehension or description!—And, although men of *uncultivated* minds, and even some *learned* individuals, (but in this one point blinded by *prejudice*,) readily choose, as the object of their adoration, any thing which they can always see, and which they pretend to *feel*; the absurdity of such conduct is not thereby in the least degree diminished.

My constant reflections on the inconvenient, or rather injurious rites, introduced by the peculiar practice of Hindoo idolatry, which, more than any other Pagan worship, destroys the texture of society, together with compassion for my countrymen, have compelled me to use every possible effort to awaken them from their dream of error: and by making them acquainted with their scriptures, enable them to contemplate with true devotion the unity and omnipresence of Nature's God.

By taking the path which conscience and sincerity direct, I, born a Brahmun, have exposed myself to the complainings and reproaches, even of some of my relations, whose prejudices are strong, and whose temporal advantage depends upon the present system. But these, however accumulated, I can tranquilly bear; trusting that a day will arrive when my humble endeavours will be viewed with justice—perhaps acknowledged with gratitude. At any rate, whatever men may say, I cannot be deprived of this consolation: my motives are acceptable to that Being who beholds in secret and compensates openly!

ABRIDGMENT

OF

THE VEDANT.

The illustrious Byas,* in his celebrated work, the Vedant, insinuates in the first text, that it is absolutely necessary for mankind to acquire knowledge respecting the Supreme Being, who is the subject of discourse in all the Veds, and the Vedant, as well as in the other Systems of Theology. But he found, from the following passages of the Veds, that this inquiry is limited to very narrow bounds, *viz.* "The Supreme Being is not "comprehensible by vision, or by any other of the or-"gans of sense; nor can he be conceived by means of "devotion, or virtuous practices!"† "He sees every "thing, though never seen; hears every thing, though "never directly heard of! He is neither short, nor is "he long;‡ inaccessible to the reasoning faculty; not "to be compassed by description; beyond the limits of "the explanation of the Ved, or of human conception!"§ Byas, also, from the result of various arguments coin-

* The greatest of the Indian theologists, philosophers, and poets, was begotten by the celebrated Purasur and Sutyubutee. Byas collected and divided the Veds into certain books and chapters, he is therefore commonly called Vedu Byas. The word Byas is composed of the preposition *bi* and the verb *uss* to divide.

† Munduc. ‡ Brih'darunnuc. § Cuthubulli.

ciding with the Ved, found that the accurate and positive knowledge of the Supreme Being is not within the boundary of comprehension; *i. e.* that *what*, and *how*, the Supreme Being is, cannot be definitely ascertained. He has therefore, in the second text, explained the Supreme Being by his effects and works, without attempting to define his essence; in like manner as we, not knowing the real nature of the sun, explain him to be the cause of the succession of days and epochs. "He "by whom the birth, existence, and annihilation of the "world is regulated, is the Supreme Being!" We see the multifarious, wonderful universe, as well as the birth, existence, and annihilation, of its different parts; hence, we naturally infer the existence of a being who regulates the whole, and call him the Supreme: in the same manner as from the sight of a pot, we conclude the existence of its artificer. The Ved, in like manner, declares the Supreme Being thus: "He from whom the universal "world proceeds, who is the Lord of the Universe, and "whose work is the universe, is the Supreme Being!"*

The *Ved* is not supposed to be an eternal Being, though sometimes dignified with such an epithet; because its being created by the Supreme Being is declared in the same Ved thus: "All the texts and parts "of the Ved were created:" and also in the third text of the Vedant, God is declared to be the cause of all the Veds.

The *void Space* is not conceived to be the independent cause of the world, notwithstanding the following declaration of the Ved, "The world proceeds from the "void space;"† for the Ved again declares, "By the

* Taittureeu. † Chhandoggu.

" Supreme Being the void space was produced." And the Vedant* says: " As the Supreme Being is evi-" dently declared in the Ved to be the cause of the " void Space, Air, and Fire, neither of them can be " supposed to be the independent cause of the uni-" verse."

Neither is *Air* allowed to be the Lord of the Universe, although the Ved says in one instance, " In Air " every existing creature is absorbed;" for the Ved again affirms, that " Breath, the intellectual power, all " the internal and external senses, the void Space, Air, " Light, Water, and the extensive Earth, proceeded " from the Supreme Being!" The Vedant† also says: " God is meant by the following text of the Ved, as " a Being more extensive than all the extension of " Space;" *viz.* " *That* breath is greater than the exten-" sion of Space in all directions," as it occurs in the Ved, after the discourse concerning common breath is concluded.

Light, of whatever description, is not inferred to be the Lord of the Universe, from the following assertion of the Ved: " The pure Light of all Lights is the Lord " of all creatures;" for the Ved again declares,‡ that " The sun and all others imitate God, and borrow their " light from him;" and the same declaration is found in the Vedant.§

Neither can *Nature* be construed by the following texts of the Ved, to be the independent cause of the world: *viz.* " Man having known *that* Nature which is " an eternal being, without a beginning or an end, is

* Fourteenth text, 4th sec. 1st chap. † 8th, 3d, 1st.

‡ Moonduc. § 22d, 3d, 1st.

"delivered from the grasp of death!" and, "Nature "operates herself!" because the Ved affirms that "No "being is superior or equal to God!"* and the Ved commands, "Know God alone!"† and the Vedant‡ thus declares: "Nature is not the Creator of the world, "not being represented so by the Ved," for it expressly says, "God has by his sight created the Universe." Nature is an insensible Being, she is, therefore, void of sight or intention, and consequently unable to create the regular world.§

Atoms are not supposed to be the cause of the world, notwithstanding the following declaration: "This "(Creator) is the most minute Being." Because an atom is an insensible particle, and from the above authority it is proved, that no Being void of understanding can be the author of a system so skilfully arranged.

The *Soul* cannot be inferred from the following texts, to be the Lord of the Universe, nor the independent Ruler of the intellectual powers; *viz.* "The Soul being joined "to the resplendent Being, enjoys by itself," "God and "the Soul enter the small void space of the heart;" because the Ved declares that "He (God) resides in the Soul as its Ruler," and that "The Soul being joined to the "gracious Being, enjoys happiness."‖ The Vedant also says, "The sentient soul is not understood to reside as "ruler in the Earth, because in both texts of the Ved "it is differently declared from that Being who rules the "Earth:" *viz.* "He (God) resides in the faculty of the "understanding," and "He, who resides in the Soul, "&c."

* Cuthu. † Moonduc. ‡ 5th, 1st, 1st.
§ Cuthu. ‖ 20th, 2d, 1st.

No *God* or *Goddess of the Earth* can be meant by the following text, as the ruler of the Earth, *viz.* * "He "who resides in the Earth, and is distinct from the Earth, "and whom the Earth does not know," &c.: because the Ved affirms that, "This (God alone) is the ruler of "internal sense, and is the eternal Being;" and the same is asserted in the Vedant.†

By the text which begins with the following sentence: *viz.* "This is the Sun," and by several other texts testifying the dignity of the sun, he is not supposed to be the original cause of the universe, because the Ved declares, that‡ "He who resides in the Sun (as his Lord) "is distinct from the Sun," and the Vedant declares the same.§

In like manner none of the celestial Gods can be inferred from the various assertions of the Ved, respecting their deities respectively, to be the independent cause of the Universe; because the Ved repeatedly affirms, that "All the Veds prove nothing but the unity of the "Supreme Being." By allowing the Divinity more than one Being, the following positive affirmations of the Ved, relative to the unity of God, become false and absurd: "God is indeed one and has no second."|| "There is none but the Supreme Being possessed of "universal knowledge."¶ "He who is without any "figure, and beyond the limit of description, is the "Supreme Being."** "Appellations and figures of all "kinds are innovations." And from the authority of many other texts it is evident that any being that bears

* Brih'darunnue. † 18th, 2d, 1st. ‡ Brih'darunnue.
§ 21st, 1st, 1st. || Cuthu. ¶ Brih'darunnue.
** Chhandoggu.

figure, and is subject to description, cannot be the eternal independent cause of the universe.

The Veds not only call the celestial representations Deities, but also in many instances give the divine epithet to the mind, diet, void space, quadruped animal, slaves, and flymen: as, "The Supreme Being is a quadruped animal in one place, and in another he is full of glory. The mind is the Supreme Being, it is to be worshipped," "God is the letter ku as well as khu," and "God is in the shape of slaves and that of flymen." The Ved has allegorically represented God in the figure of the Universe, *viz.* "Fire is his head, the sun and the moon are his two eyes,"* &c. And also the Ved calls God the void space of the heart, and declares him to be smaller than the grain of paddy and barley: but from the foregoing quotations neither any of the celestial Gods, nor any existing creature, should be considered the Lord of the Universe, because the † third chapter of the Vedant explains the reason for these secondary assertions thus: "By these appellations of the Ved which denote the diffusive spirit of the Supreme Being equally over all creatures by means of extension, his omnipresence is established:" so the Ved says, "All that exists is indeed God,"‡ *i. e.* nothing bears true existence excepting God, "and whatever we smell or taste is the Supreme Being," *i. e.* the existence of whatever thing that appears to us relies on the existence of God. It is indisputably evident that none of these metaphorical representations, which arise from the elevated style in which all the Veds are written, were designed to be viewed in any

* Monduc. † 38th text, 2d sec. ‡ Chhanddoggu.

other light than mere allegory. Should individuals be acknowledged to be separate deities, there would be a necessity for acknowledging many independent creators of the world, which is directly contrary to common sense, and to the repeated authority of the Ved. The Vedant* also declares, "That Being which is distinct "from matter, and from those which are contained in "matter, is not various, because he is declared by all the "Veds to be one beyond description;" and it is again stated that "The Ved has declared the Supreme Being "to be mere understanding;"† also in the third chapter is found that, "The Ved having at first explained the "Supreme Being by different epithets, begins with the "word *Uthu*, or now," and declares that "All descrip-"tions which I have used to describe the Supreme "Being are incorrect," because he by no means can be described; and so is it stated in the sacred commentaries of the Ved.

The fourteenth text of the second sect. of the third chapter of the Vedant declares, "It being directly re-"presented by the Ved, that the Supreme Being bears "no figure nor form;" and the following texts of the Ved assert the same, *viz*. "That true Being was before "all."‡ "The Supreme Being has no feet, but extends "every were; has no hands, yet holds every thing; has "no eyes, yet sees all that is; has no ears, yet hears "every thing that passes." "His existence had no "cause." "He is the smallest of the small, and the "greatest of the great: and yet is, in fact, neither "small nor great!"

* 11th 2d, 3d. † 16th, 2d, 3d. ‡ Chhandoggu.

In answer to the following questions, *viz.* How can the Supreme Being be supposed to be distinct from, and above all existing creatures, and at the same time omnipresent? How is it possible that he should be described by properties inconceivable by reason, as seeing without eye, and hearing without ear? To these questions the Vedant, in chapter second, replies, "In God are all "sorts of power and splendour." And the following passages of the Ved also declare the same: "God is all-"powerful;"* and "It is by his supremacy that he is in "possession of all powers;" *i. e.* what may be impossible for us is not impossible for God, who is the Almighty, and the sole regulator of the Universe.

Some celestial Gods have, in different instances, declared themselves to be independent deities, and also the object of worship; but these declarations were owing to their thoughts being abstracted from themselves and their being entirely absorbed in divine reflection.† The Vedant declares: "This exhortation of Indru (or "the god of atmosphere) respecting his divinity, to be "indeed agreeable to the authorities of the Ved;" that is, "Every one, on having lost all self-consideration "in consequence of being united with divine reflection, "may speak as assuming to be the Supreme Being; "like Bamdev (a celebrated Brahmun) who, in conse-"quence of such self-forgetfulness, declared himself to "have created the Sun, and Munoo the next person to "Brahma." It is therefore optional with every one of the celestial Gods, as well as with every individual, to consider himself as God, under this state of self-forget-

* Shyetashyutur.

† 30th, 1st, 1st.

fulness and unity with the divine reflection, as the Ved says, " you are that true Being" (when you lose all self-consideration), and " O God I am nothing but you." The sacred commentators have made the same observation, *viz.* " I am nothing but true Being, and am pure " Understanding, full of eternal happiness, and am " by nature free from worldly effects." But in consequence of this reflection, none of them can be acknowledged to be the cause of the universe or the object of adoration.

God is the efficient cause of the universe, as a potter is of earthen pots; and he is also the material cause of it, the same as the earth is the material cause of the different earthen pots, or as a rope, at an inadvertent view taken for a snake, is the material cause of the conceived existence of the Snake, which appears to be true by the support of the real existence of the rope. So says the Vedant,* " God is the efficient cause of the " Universe, as well as the material cause thereof (as a " spider of its web), as the Ved has positively declared, " That from a knowledge of God alone, a knowledge " of every existing thing proceeds." Also the Ved compares the knowledge respecting the Supreme Being to a knowledge of the earth, and the knowledge respecting the different species existing in the universe, to the knowledge of earthen pots, which declaration and comparison prove the unity between the Supreme Being and the universe; and by the following declarations of the Ved, *viz.* " The Supreme Being has by his sole " intention created the Universe," it is evident that God is the wilful agent of all that can have existence.

* 23d, 8th, 1st.

As the Ved says that the Supreme Being intended (at the time of creation) to extend himself, it is evident that the Supreme Being is the origin of all matter, and its various appearances; as the reflection of the sun's meridian rays on sandy plains is the cause of the resemblance of an extended sea. The Ved says, "That "all figures and their appellations are mere inventions, "and that the Supreme Being alone is real existence," consequently things that bear figure and appellation cannot be supposed the cause of the universe.

The following texts of the Ved, *viz.* "Crishnu (the god "of preservation) is greater than all the celestial gods, "to whom the mind should be applied." "We all "worship Muhadev (the god of destruction)." "We "adore the sun." "I worship the most revered Buron "(the god of the sea)." "Dost thou worship me, says "Air, who am the eternal and universal life." "Intel-"lectual power is God, which should be adored;" "and Oodgueet (or a certain part of the Ved) should be "worshipped." These, as well as several other texts of the same nature, are not real commands to worship the persons and things above-mentioned, but only direct those who are unfortunately incapable of adoring the invisible Supreme Being, to apply their minds to any visible thing, rather than allow them to remain idle. The Vedant also states, that "The declaration of the "Ved,"* "that those who worship the celestial gods are "the food of such gods," is an allegorical expression, and only means that they are comforts to the celestial gods, as food is to mankind; for he who has no faith in

* 7th, 1st, 3d.

the Supreme Being is rendered subject to these gods. The Ved affirms the same: *viz.* "He who worships "any god, excepting the Supreme Being, and thinks "that he is distinct and inferior to that god, knows "nothing, and is considered as a domestic beast of "these gods." And the Vedant also asserts; *viz.* "The worship authorized by all the Veds is of one "nature, as the directions for the worship of the only "Supreme Being is invariably found in every part "of the Ved; and the epithets the Supreme and "the Omnipresent Being, &c. commonly imply God "alone."*

The following passages of the Ved affirm that God is the sole object of worship, *viz.*† "adore God alone." "Know God alone; give up all other discourse." And the Vedant says, that "It is found in the Veds,‡ 'That 'none but the Supreme Being is to be worshipped, 'nothing excepting him should be adored by a wise 'man.'"

Moreover, the Vedant declares that "Byas is of "opinion that the adoration of the Supreme Being is "required of mankind as well of the celestial gods; "because the possibility of self-resignation to God is "equally observed in both mankind and the celestial "deities."§ The Ved also states,|| that "Of the celestial "gods, of the pious Brahmuns, and of men in general, "that person who understands and believes the Al- "mighty Being, will be absorbed in him." It is therefore concluded that the celestial gods and mankind have an equal duty in divine worship; and besides it is

* 1st, 3d, 3d. † Brehdarunnuc. ‡ 67th, 3d, 3d.
§ 26th, 3d, 1st. || Brehdarunnuc.

proved from the following authority of the Ved, that any man who adores the Supreme Being is adored by all the celestial gods, *viz.* "All the celestial gods wor-"ship him who applies his mind to the Supreme "Being."*

The Ved now illustrates the mode in which we should worship the Supreme Being, *viz.* "To God we should "approach, of him we should hear, of him we should "think, and to him we should attempt to approxi-"mate."† The Vedant also elucidates the subject thus: "The three latter directions in the above quoted text, "are conducive to the first, *viz.* 'Approaching to "God.'" These three are in reality included in the first (as the direction for collecting fire in the worship of fire), for we cannot approach to God without hearing and thinking of him, nor without attempting to make our approximation; and the last, *viz.* attempting to approximate to God, is required until we have approached him. By hearing of God is meant hearing his declarations, which establish his unity; and by thinking of him is meant thinking of the contents of his law; and by attempting to approximate to him is meant attempting to apply our minds to that true Being on which the diffusive existence of the universe relies, in order that by means of the constant practice of this attempt we may approach to him. The Vedant states,‡ that "Constant practice of devotion is necessary, it "being represented so by the Ved;" and also adds that "We should adore God till we approach to him, "and even then not forsake his adoration, such "authority being found in the Ved."

* Chhandoggu. † 47th, 4th, 3d. ‡ 1st, 1st, 4th.

The Vedant shews that moral principle is a part of the adoration of God, *viz.* "A command over our "passions and over the external senses of the body "and good acts, are declared by the Ved to be indis-"pensable in the mind's approximation to God, they "should therefore be strictly taken care of, and attended "to, both previously and subsequently to such approxi-"mation to the Supreme Being;"* *i. e.* we should not indulge our evil propensities, but should endeavour to have entire control over them. Reliance on, and self-resignation to, the only true Being, with an aversion to worldly considerations, are included in the good acts above alluded to. The adoration of the Supreme Being produces eternal beatitude, as well as all desired advantages; as the Vedant declares: "It is the firm "opinion of Byas that from devotion to God all the "desired consequences proceed;"† and it is thus often represented by the Ved, "He who is desirous of pros-"perity should worship the Supreme Being."‡ "He "who knows God thoroughly adheres unto God." "The souls of the deceased forefathers of him who "adores the true Being alone, enjoy freedom by his "mere wish."§ "All the celestial gods worship him "who applies his mind to the Supreme Being;" and "He, who sincerely adores the Supreme Being, is "exempted from further transmigration."

A pious householder is entitled to the adoration of God equally with an Uti:‖ The Vedant says, that

* 27th, 4th, 3d. † 1st, 4th, 3d. ‡ Monduc. § Chhandoggu.

‖ The highest among the four sects of Brahmuns, who, according to the religious order, are bound to forsake all worldly considerations, and to spend their time in the sole adoration of God.

" A householder may be allowed the performance of all " the ceremonies attached to the (Brahminical) religion, " and also the fulfilling of the devotion of God: the " fore-mentioned mode of worshipping the Supreme " Being, therefore, is required of a householder pos- " sessed of moral principles."* And the Ved declares, " That the celestial gods, and householders of strong " faith, and professional uttis, are alike."

It is optional to those who have faith in God alone. to observe and attend to the rules and rites prescribed by the Ved, applicable to the different classes of Hindoos, and to their different religious orders respectively. But in case of the true believers neglecting those rites, they are not liable to any blame whatever; as the Vedant says, " Before acquiring the true knowledge of " God, it is proper for man to attend to the laws and " rules laid down by the Ved for different classes, " according to their different professions; because the " Ved declares the performance of these rules to be the " cause of the mind's purification, and its faith in " God, and compares it with a saddle-horse, which " helps a man to arrive at the wished-for goal."† And the Vedant also says, that " Man may acquire the true " knowledge of God even without observing the rules " and rites prescribed by the Ved for each class of Hin- " doos, as it is found in the Ved that many persons " who had neglected the performance of the Brahmini- " cal rites and ceremonies, owing to their perpetual " attention to the adoration of the Supreme Being, ac- " quired the true knowledge respecting the Deity."‡

* 28th, 4th, 3d. † 36th, 4th, 3d. ‡ 36th, 4th, 3d.

The Vedant again more clearly states that, "It is "equally found in the Ved that some people, though "they had their entire faith in God alone, yet per-"formed both the worship of God and the ceremonies "prescribed by the Ved; and that some others neg-"lected them, and merely worshipped God."* The following texts of the Ved fully explain the subject, *viz.* "Junuku (one of the noted devotees) had per-"formed Yugnyu (or the adoration of the celestial "gods through fire) with the gift of a considerable "sum of money, as a fee to the holy Brahmuns," and "many learned true believers never worshipped fire, "nor any celestial god through fire."

Notwithstanding it is optional with those who have their faith in the only God, to attend to the prescribed ceremonies or to neglect them entirely, the Vedant prefers the former to the latter, because the Ved says that attendance to the religious ceremonies conduces to the attainment of the Supreme Being.

Although the Ved says, "That he who has true faith "in the omnipresent Supreme Being may eat all that "exists,"† *i. e.* is not bound to enquire what is his food, or who prepares it, nevertheless the Vedant limits that authority thus: "The above-mentioned authority of the "Ved for eating all sorts of food should only be ob-"served at the time of distress, because it is found in "the Ved, that Chacraunu (a celebrated Brahmun) ate "the meat cooked by the elephant-keepers during a "famine."‡ It is concluded, that he acted according to the above stated authority of the Ved, only at the time of distress.

Devotion to the Supreme Being is not limited to any

* 9th, 4th, 3d. † Chhandoggu. ‡ 28th, 4th, 3d.

holy place or sacred country, as the Vedant says, "In "any place wherein the mind feels itself undisturbed, "men should worship God; because no specific au- "thority for the choice of any particular place of wor- "ship is found in the Ved,"* which declares, "In "any place which renders the mind easy, man should "adore God."

It is of no consequence to those who have true belief in God, whether they die while the sun is in the north or south of the equator, as the Vedant declares, "That any one who has faith in the only God, dying "even when the sun may be south of the equator,† his "soul shall proceed from the body, through Soo khumna "(a vein which, as the Brahmuns suppose, passes through "the navel up to the brain), and approaches to the Su- "preme Being.‡" The Ved also positively asserts "That "he, who in life was devoted to the Supreme Being, "shall (after death) be absorbed in him, and again be "neither liable to birth nor death, reduction nor aug- "mentation."

The Ved begins and concludes with the three peculiar and mysterious epithets of God, *viz.* first, ONG; second, TUT; third, SUT. The first of these signifies "*That* Being, which preserves, destroys, and creates!" The second implies "*That* only being, which is neither "male nor female!" The third announces "*The true being!*" These collective terms simply affirm, that ONE, UNKNOWN, TRUE BEING, IS THE CREATOR, PRESERVER, AND DESTROYER OF THE UNIVERSE!!!

* 11th, 1st, 4th.

† It is believed by the Brahmuns, that any one who dies while the sun is south of the equator, cannot enjoy eternal beatitude.

‡ 20th, 2d, 4th.

TRANSLATION

OF THE

MOONDUK-OPUNISHUD

OF THE

UTHURVU-VED,

ACCORDING TO THE GLOSS OF THE CELEBRATED

SHUNKURA-CHARYU.

CALCUTTA:
1819.

INTRODUCTION.

DURING the intervals between my controversial engagements with idolators as well as with advocates for idolatry, I translated several of the ten Oopunishuds, of which the Vedantu or principal part of the Veds consists, and of which the Shareeruk-Meemangsa, commonly called the Vedant-Durshun, composed by the celebrated Vyas, is explanatory; I have now taken the opportunity of further leisure to publish a translation of the Moonduk-Opunishud. An attentive perusal of this, as well as of the remaining books of the Vedantu, will, I trust, convince every unprejudiced mind, that they, with great consistency, inculcate the unity of God; instructing men, at the same time, in the pure mode of adoring him in spirit. It will also appear evident that the Veds, although they tolerate idolatry as the last provision for those who are totally incapable of raising their minds to the contemplation of the invisible God of nature, yet repeatedly urge the relinquishment of the rites of idol worship, and the adoption of a purer system of religion, on the express grounds, that the observance of idolatrous rites can never be productive of eternal beatitude. These are left to be practised by such persons only as, notwithstanding the constant teaching of spiritual guides, cannot be brought to see perspicuously the majesty of God through the works of nature.

The public will, I hope, be assured that nothing but the natural inclination of the ignorant towards the worship of objects resembling their own nature, and to the external forms of rites palpable to their grosser senses, joined to the self-interested motives of their pretended guides, has rendered the generality of the Hindoo community (in defiance of their sacred books) devoted to idol worship;—the source of prejudice and superstition, and of the total destruction of moral principle, as countenancing criminal intercourse,* suicide,† female murder,‡ and human sacrifice. Should my labeurs prove in any degree the means of diminishing the extent of those evils, I shall ever deem myself most amply rewarded.

* Vide Defence of Hindoo Theism.

† Vide Introduction to the Cena-Upanishad.

‡ Vide Treatise on Widow-burning.

THE

MOONDUK-OPUNISHUD

OF THE

UTHURVU-VED.

BRUHMA, the greatest of celestial deities, and executive creator and preserver of the world, came into form; he instructed Uthurvu, his eldest son, in the knowledge respecting the Supreme Being, on which all sciences rest. Uthurvu communicated formerly to Ungir what Bruhmá taught him: Ungir imparted the same knowledge to one of the descendants of Bhurudwaju, *called* Sutyuvahu, who conveyed the doctrine so handed down to Ungirus. Shounuku, a wealthy householder, having in the prescribed manner approached Ungirus, asked, " Is there any being by whose knowledge alone the whole universe may be *immediately* known? He (*Ungirus*) then replied: " Those who have a thorough knowledge of the Veds, say that it should be understood that there are two sorts of knowledge; one superior, and the other inferior: There are the Rig-ved, Ujoor-ved, Samu-ved, and Uthurvu-ved; and also *their subordinate parts, consisting of* Shiksha, or a treatise on pronunciation; Kulpu, or the science that teaches the details of rites according to the different branches of the Veds; Vyákurnu, or grammar; Nirookti, or explanation of the peculiar terms of the Veds; Ch,hundus, or prosody; and Jyotish, or astronomy: *which all* belong to the inferior kind of knowledge. Now the superior kind *is conveyed by the Oopunishuds and* is that through which absorption into the eternal Supreme Being may be obtained. That Supreme Being *who is the subject of the superior learning*, is beyond the apprehension of the senses, and out of the reach of the corporeal organs of action, and is without origin, colour, or magnitude; and has neither eye nor ear, nor has he hand or foot. He is everlasting, all-pervading, omnipresent, absolutely incorporeal, unchangeable, and it is he whom wise men consider as the origin of the universe;—In the same way as the cobweb is created and absorbed by the spider *independently of exterior origin*, as vegetables proceed from the earth, and hair and nails from animate creatures, so the Universe is produced by the eternal Supreme Being.

From his omniscience the Supreme Being resolves to create the Universe;—Then nature, *the apparent cause of the world*, is produced by him;—From her the prior operating sensitive particle of the world, styled Bruhmá, the source of the faculties, proceeds. *From the faculties* the five elements *are produced; thence spring* the *seven* divisions of the world, whereon ceremonial rites, with their consequences, are brought forth. By him who knows all things, collectively and distinctly, whose knowledge and will are the only means of all his actions, Bruhmá, name, and form, and all that vegetates are produced.

End of the first Section of the 1st Moondukum.

Those rites,* the prescription of which wise men, *such as Vushisthu, and others* found in the Veds, are truly the means *of producing good consequences.* They have been performed in various manners by three sects among Brahmuns, *namely, Udhuryoo, or those who are well versed in the Ujoor-ved; Oodgata, or the sect who know thoroughly the Samu-ved; and Hota, those Bruhmuns that have a perfect knowledge of the Rig-ved.* You all continue to perform them, as long as you feel a desire to enjoy gratifications attainable from them. This practice of performing rites is the way which leads you to the benefits you expect to derive from your works.

Fire being augmented when its flame waves, *the observer of rites* shall offer oblations to deities in the middle of the waving flame.

If observance of the sacred fire be not attended with the rites required to be performed on the days of new and full moon, and during the four months of the rains, and in the autumn and spring; and be also not attended with hospitality and due regard to time or the worship of Vushyudevu, and be fulfilled without regard to prescribed forms, it will deprive the worshipper of the enjoyments which he might otherwise expect in his seven future mansions.

Kalee, Kuralee, Munojuvá, Soolo-hitá, Soodho-omruvurná, Sphoolinginee, Veshwuroochee, are the *seven names of the* seven waving points of the flame.

He who offers oblations at the prescribed time in

* In the beginning of this section, the author treats of the subject of the inferior knowledge; and in the conclusion he introduces that of the superior doctrine, which he continues throughout the whole Oopunishud.

those illuminating and waving points of fire, is carried by the oblations so offered through the rays of the Sun to the Heaven where Indru, prince of the celestial gods, reigns. The illuminating oblations, while carrying the observer of rites through the rays of the Sun, *invite him* to heaven, *saying*, " Come in ! come in !" and entertaining him with pleasing conversation, and treating him with veneration, say to him, " This is the summit of the heavens, the fruit of your good works."

The eighteen members of rites and sacrifices, *void of the true knowledge*, are infirm and perishable: Those ignorant persons who consider them as the source of real bliss, shall, after the enjoyment of future gratification, undergo transmigations. Those fools who, immersed in ignorance, *that is, the foolish practice of rites*, consider themselves to be wise and learned, wander about, repeatedly subjecting themselves to *birth, disease, death, and other* pains, like blind men when guided by a blind *man*.

Engaged in various manners of rites and sacrifices, the ignorant are sure of obtaining their objects: but as the observers of such rites, from their excessive desire of fruition, remain destitute of a knowledge of God, they, afflicted with sorrows, descend to this world after the time of their celestial gratification is expired. Those complete fools believe, that the rites prescribed by the Veds in performing sacrifices, and those laid down by the Smrities at the digging of wells and other pious liberal actions, are the most beneficial, and have no idea that a knowledge *of, and faith in God*, are the only true sources of bliss: They after death, having enjoyed the consequence of such rites on the summit of heaven, transmigrate in the human form, or in that of inferior animals, or of plants.

Mendicants and hermits, who residing in forests, live upon alms, as well as *householders* possessed of a portion of wisdom, practising religious austerities, the worship of Brahmá and others, and exercising a control over the senses, freed from sins, ascend through the northern path* to the highest part of heaven, where the immortal Brahmá, who is coeval with the world, assumes *his supremacy*.

Having taken into serious consideration the perishable nature of all objects *within the world*, which are acquirable from human works, a Brahmun shall cease to desire them; reflecting within himself, that nothing *which is obtained through perishable means* can be expected to be eternal: hence what use of rites? He then, with a view to acquire a knowledge of superior learning, shall proceed, with a load of wood in his hand, to a spiritual teacher who is versed in the doctrines of the Veds, and has firm faith in God. The wise teacher shall properly instruct his pupil so devoted to him, freed from the importunities of external senses, and possessed of tranquillity of mind, in the knowledge through which he may know the eternal Supreme Being.

End of the first Moondukum.

* According to Hindoo theologians, there are two roads that lead to distinct heavens, one northern, the other southern. The former is the path to the habitation of Bruhma and the superior gods, and the latter to the heaven of Indru and the other inferior deities.

He, *the subject of the superior knowledge*, alone is true. As from a blazing fire thousands of sparks of the same nature proceed, so from the eternal Supreme Being (O beloved pupil) various souls come forth, and again they return into him.—He is immortal, and without form or figure, omnipresent, pervading external and internal objects, unborn, without breath or individual mind, pure and superior to eminently exalted nature.

From him the first sensitive particle, or the seed of the universe, individual intellect, all the senses and their *objects*, also vacuum, air, light, water, and the earth which contains all things, proceed.

Heaven is his head, and the Sun and Moon are his eyes; space is his ears, the celebrated Veds are his speech; air is his breath, the world is his intellect, and the earth is his feet; *for* he is the soul of the whole universe.

By him the sky, which is illuminated by the Sun, *is produced;* clouds, which have their origin from the effects of the Moon, *accumulating them in the sky,* bring forth vegetables in the earth; Man imparts the essence *drawn from these vegetables*, to Woman; *then through the combination of such physical causes*, numerous offspring come forth from the omnipresent Supreme Being.

From him all the texts of the Veds, consisting of verses, musical compositions, and prose, proceed; *in like manner by him* are produced Deeksha, or certain preliminary ceremonies, and sacrifices, without sacrificial posts or with them; *fees* lastly, offered in sacrifices, time, and the principal person who institutes the performance of sacrifices and defrays their expences;

as well as future mansions, where the Moon effects purification and where the Sun *shines.*—By him Gods of several descriptions, all celestial beings subordinate to those Gods, mankind, animals, birds, both breath and peditum, wheat and barley, austerity, conviction, truth, duties of ascetics, and *rules* for conducting human life, were created.—From him seven individual senses within the head proceed, as well as their seven respective inclinations towards their objects, their seven objects, and ideas acquired through them, and their seven organs *(two eyes, two ears, the two passages of nose and mouth)*, in which those senses are situated in every living creature, and which never cease to act except at the time of sleep.

From him, oceans and all mountains proceed, and various rivers flow: all vegetables, tastes, *(consisting of sweet, salt, pungent, bitter, sour, and astringent)* united with which the visible elementary substance encloses the corpuscle situate in the heart.*—The Supreme existence is himself all—rites as well as their rewards: He therefore is the Supreme and Immortal: He who knows him (O beloved Pupil) as residing in the hearts *of all animate Beings*, disentangles the knot of ignorance in this world.

End of the first section of the second Moondukum.

* This corpuscle is supposed to be constituted of all the various elements that enter into the composition of the animal frame. Within it the soul has its residence, and acting upon it, operates through its medium in the whole system. To this corpuscle the soul remains attached through all changes of being, until finally absorbed into the supreme intelligence.

God, as being resplendent and most proximate *to all creatures*, is styled the operator in the heart; he is great and all-sustaining; for on him rest all existences, such as those that move, those that breathe, those that twinkle, and those that do not. Such is God. You all contemplate him as the support of all objects, visible and invisible, the chief end *of human pursuit.* He surpasses all human understanding, and is the most pre-eminent. He, who irradiates *the Sun and other bodies*, who is smaller than an atom, larger *than the world*, and in whom is the abode of all the divisions of the universe, and of all their inhabitants, is the eternal God; the origin of breath, speech, and intellect, as well *as of all the senses*. He, *the origin of all the senses*, the true and unchangeable Supreme Being, should be meditated upon; and do thou (O beloved pupil) apply constantly thy mind to him. Seizing the bow found in the Oopunishuds, the strongest of weapons, man shall draw the arrow *(of the soul)*, sharpened by the constant application of mind *to God.* Do thou (O pupil), *being in the same practice*, withdrawing all *the senses from worldly objects*, through the mind directed towards the Supreme Being, hit the mark which is the eternal God. The word Om, *signifying God*, is represented as the bow, the Soul as the arrow, and the Supreme Being as its aim, which a man of steady mind should hit: he then shall be united to God as the arrow to its mark. In God, heaven, earth, and space reside, and also intellect, with breath and all the senses. Do you strive to know solely the ONE Supreme Being, and forsake all other discourse; because this *(a true knowledge respect-*

ing God) is the only way to eternal beatitude. The veins of the body are inserted into the heart, like the radius of a wheel into its nave. There the Supreme Being, as the origin of the notion of individuality, and of its various circumstances, resides; Him through the help of Om, you all contemplate. Blessed be ye in crossing over the ocean of dark ignorance to absorption into God. He who knows the universe collectively and distinctively, whose majesty is fully evident in the world, operates within the space of the heart, his luminous abode.

He is perceptible only by intellect; and removes the breath and corpuscle, *in which the soul resides*, from one substance to another; supporting intellectual faculties, he is seated in the heart: Wise men acquire a knowledge of him, who shines eternal, and the source of all happiness, through the pure knowledge *conveyed to them by the Veds and by spiritual fathers.*—God, who is all in all, being known to man as the origin of intellect and self-consciousness, every desire of the mind ceases, all doubts are removed, and effects of the good or evil actions committed, now or in preceding shapes, are totally annihilated. The Supreme Being, free from stain, devoid of figure or form, and entirely pure, the light of all lights, resides in the heart, his resplendently excellent seat: those *discriminating* men, who know him *as the origin of intellect and of self-consciousness*, are possessed of the real notion of God. Neither the sun nor the moon, nor yet the stars, can throw light on God: even the illuminating lightning cannot throw light upon him, much less can limited fire give him light: but they all imitate him, and all borrow their light from him.—God alone is immortal: he extends before, behind, to the right, to the left, beneath and above. He is the Supreme, and all in all.

End of the 2d Moondukum.

Two birds *(meaning God and the soul)*, cohabitant and co-essential, reside unitedly in one tree, *which is the body.* One of them *(the soul)* consumes the variously tasted fruits of its actions; but the other *(God)*, without partaking of them, witnesses *all events.*

The soul so pressed down in the body, being deluded with ignorance, grieves at its own insufficiency; but when it perceives its cohabitant, the adorable Lord *of the universe,** the origin of itself, and his glory, it feels relieved from grief and infatuation. When a wise man perceives the resplendent God, the Creator and Lord *of the universe,* and the omnipresent prime cause, he then, abandoning the consequences of good and evil works, becomes perfect, and obtains entire absorption. A wise man knowing God as perspicuously residing in all creatures, forsakes all idea of duality; *being convinced that there is only one real existence, which is God.* He then directs all his senses towards God alone, the origin of self-consciousness, and on him exclusively he places his love, abstracting at the same time his mind

* The difference between God, the intellectual principle, and the Soul, the individual intellect, subsists as long as the idea of self-individuality is retained; like the distinction between finite and infinite space, which ceases as soon as the idea of particular figure is done away.

from all worldly objects by constantly applying it to God: the person so devoted is reckoned the most perfect among the votaries of the Deity.—Through strict veracity, the uniform direction of mind and senses, and through notions acquired from spiritual teachers, as well as by abstinence from sexual indulgence, Man should approach God, who, full of splendour and perfection, works in the heart; and to whom only the votaries freed from passion and desire can approximate.

He who practises veracity prospers, and not he who speaks untruths: the way to eternal beatitude is open to him who without omission speaketh truth. This is that way through which the saints, extricated from all desires, proceed to the supreme existence, the consequence of the observance of truth. He is great and incomprehensible by the senses, and consequently his nature is beyond human conception. He, though more subtle than vacuum itself, shines in various ways —*From those who do not know him*, he is at a greater distance than the limits of space, and *to those who acquire a knowledge of him*, he is most proximate; and while residing in animate creatures he is perceived obscurely *by those who apply their thoughts to him.* He is not perceptible by vision, nor is he describable by means of speech: neither can he be the object of any of the other organs of sense; nor can he be conceived by the help of austerities or religious rites: but a person whose mind is purified by the light of true knowledge, through incessant contemplation, perceives him the most pure God. Such is the invisible Supreme Being: he should be observed in the heart, wherein breath, consisting of five species, rests. The mind being perfectly freed from impurity, God who spreads over the mind and all the senses, imparts a knowledge of himself to the heart.

A pious votary of God obtains whatever division of the world, and whatever desirable object he may wish to acquire *for himself or for another*: therefore any one, who is desirous of honour and advantage, should revere him.

End of the 1*st Section of the* 3*d Moondukhum.*

Those wise men who, abandoning all desires, revere the devotee who has acquired a knowledge of the supreme exaltation of God, on whom the whole universe rests, and who is perfect and illuminates every where, will never be subjected to further birth.

He who, contemplating the various effects of objects visible or invisible, feels a desire to obtain them, shall be born again with those feelings: but the man satisfied with a knowledge of and faith in God, blessed by a total destruction of ignorance, forsakes all such desires even during his life.

A knowledge of God, *the prime object,* is not acquirable from study of the Veds, nor through retentive memory, nor yet by continual hearing of spiritual instruction: but he who seeks to obtain a *knowledge* of God is gifted with it, God rendering himself conspicuous to him.

No man *deficient in* faith or discretion can obtain a knowledge of God; nor can even he who possesses wisdom mingled with the desire of fruition, gain it: but the soul of a wise man who, through firm belief, prudence, and pure understanding, not biassed by worldly desire, seeks for knowledge, will be absorbed into God.

The saints who, wise and firm, were satisfied solely with a knowledge of God, assured of the soul's divine origin, exempt from passion, and possessed of tranquillity of mind, having found God the omnipresent every where, have after death been absorbed into him; *even as limited extension within a jar is by its destruction united to universal space.* All the votaries who repose on God alone their firm belief, originating from a knowledge of the Vedant, and who, by forsaking religious rites, obtain purification of mind, being continually occupied in divine reflections during life, are at the time of death entirely freed from ignorance and absorbed into God. On the approach of death, the elementary parts of their body, being fifteen in number, unite with their respective origins: their corporeal faculties, *such as vision and feeling, &c.* return into their original sources, *the sun and air, &c.* The consequences of their works, together with their souls, are absorbed into the supreme and eternal spirit, *in the same manner as the reflection of the sun in water returns to him on the removal of the water.* As all rivers flowing into the ocean disappear and lose their respective appellations and forms, so the person who has acquired a knowledge of and faith in God, freeing himself from the subjugation of figure and appellation, is absorbed into the supreme immaterial and omnipresent existence.

He who acquires a knowledge of the Supreme Being *according to the foregoing doctrine*, shall inevitably be absorbed into him, *surmounting all the obstacles that he may have to encounter.* None of his progeny will be destitute of a true knowledge of God. He escapes from mental distress and from evil propensities; he is also relieved from the ignorance which occasions the idea of duality. This is the true doctrine inculcated throughout the foregoing texts, and which a man should impart to those who are accustomed to perform good works, conversant in the Veds, and inclined toward the acquisition of the knowledge of God, and who themselves, with due regard, offer oblations to sacred fire; and also to those who have continually practised Shirobrutu, *a certain observance of the sacred fire.* This is the true divine doctrine, in which Ungirus instructed *his pupil Shounuku,* which a person not accustomed to devotion should not study.

Salutation to the knowers of God!

TRANSLATION

OF THE

CÉNA UPANISHAD,

One of the Chapters of the

SÁMA VÉDA;

ACCORDING TO THE GLOSS OF THE CELEBRATED

SHANCARÁCHÁRYA:

ESTABLISHING THE

UNITY AND THE SOLE OMNIPOTENCE OF THE SUPREME BEING;

AND THAT

HE ALONE

IS THE OBJECT OF WORSHIP.

CALCUTTA:
1823.

INTRODUCTION.

SINCE my publication of the abridgment of the *Vedánta*, containing an exposition of all the *Véds* as given by the great VYAS, I have, for the purpose of illustrating and confirming the view that he has taken of them, translated into Bengalee the principal chapters of the Véds, as being of unquestionable authority amongst all Hindoos. This work will, I trust, by explaining to my countrymen the real spirit of the Hindoo Scriptures, which is but the declaration of the unity of God, tend in a great degree to correct the erroneous conceptions, which have prevailed with regard to the doctrines they inculcate. It will also, I hope, tend to discriminate those parts of the Veds which are to be interpreted in an allegorical sense, and consequently to correct those exceptionable practices, which not only deprive Hindoos in general of the common comforts* of society, but also lead them fre-

* A Hindoo of cast can only eat once between sunrise and sunset—cannot eat dressed victuals in a boat or ship—nor clothed—nor in a tavern—nor any food that has been touched by a person of a different cast—nor if interrupted while eating, can he resume his meal.

quently to self-destruction,* or to the sacrifice† of the lives of their friends and relations.

It is with no ordinary feeling of satisfaction that I have already seen many respectable persons of my countrymen, to the great disappointment of their interested spiritual guides, rise superior to their original prejudices, and enquire into the truths of religion. As many European gentlemen, especially those who interest themselves in the improvement of their fellow-creatures, may be gratified with a view of the doctrines of the original work, it appeared to me that I might best contribute to that gratification, by translating a few chapters of the Ved into the English language, which I have accordingly done, and now submit them to their candid judgment. Such benevolent people will, perhaps, rise from a perusal of them with the conviction, that in the most ancient times the inhabitants of this part of the globe (at least the more intelligent class) were not unacquainted with metaphysical subjects; that allegorical language or description was very frequently employed to represent the attributes of the Creator, which were sometimes designated as independent existences; and that, however suitable this method might be to the refined understandings of men of learning, it had the most mischievous effect when lite-

* As at Prayaga, Gunga Sagar, and under the wheels of the car of Jagannath.

† As, for instance, persons whose recovery from sickness is supposed to be doubtful, are carried to die on the banks of the Ganges. This is practised by the Hindoos of Bengal only, the cruelty of which affects even Hindoos of Behar, Ilahabad, and all the upper provinces.

rature and philosophy decayed, producing all those absurdities and idolatrous notions which have checked, or rather destroyed, every mark of reason, and darkened every beam of understanding.

The Véd from which all Hindoo literature is derived is, in the opinion of the Hindoos, an inspired work, coeval with the existence of the world. It is divided into four parts, *viz.* Rig, Yajur, Sam, and At'harva; these are again divided into several branches, and these last are subdivided into chapters. It is the general characteristic of each Véd, that the primary chapters of each branch treat of astronomy, medicine, arms, and other arts and sciences. They also exhibit allegorical representations of the attributes* of the Supreme Being, by means of earthly objects, animate or inanimate, whose shapes or properties are analogous to the nature of those attributes, and pointing out the modes of their worship, immediately, or through the medium of fire. In the subsequent chapters the unity of the Supreme Being as the sole ruler of the universe, is plainly inculcated, and the mode of worshipping him particularly directed. The doctrine of a plurality of gods and goddesses laid down in the preceding chapters is not only controverted, but reasons assigned for its introduction; for instance, that the worship of the Sun and Fire, together with the whole allegorical system, were only inculcated for the sake of those whose limited understandings rendered them incapable

* It is my intention to give, with the blessing of God, in my next publication, an account of the relation betwixt those attributes and the allegorical representations used to denote them.

of comprehending and adoring the invisible Supreme Being; so that such persons might not remain in a brutified state, destitute of all religious principles. Should this explanation given by the Véd itself, as well as by its celebrated commentator Vyas, not be allowed to reconcile those passages which are seemingly at variance with each other, as those that declare the unity of the invisible Supreme Being, with others which describe a plurality of independent visible Gods, the whole work must, I am afraid, not only be stripped of its authority, but be looked upon as altogether unintelligible.

I have often lamented that, in our general researches into theological truth, we are subjected to the conflict of many obstacles. When we look to the traditions of ancient nations, we often find them at variance with each other; and when, discouraged by this circumstance, we appeal to reason as a surer guide, we soon find how incompetent it is, alone, to conduct us to the object of our pursuit. We often find that, instead of facilitating our endeavours or clearing up our perplexities, it only serves to generate an universal doubt, incompatible with principles on which our comfort and happiness mainly depend. The best method perhaps, is, neither to give ourselves up exclusively to the guidance of the one or the other; but by a proper use of the lights furnished by both, endeavour to improve our intellectual and moral faculties, relying on the goodness of the Almighty Power, which alone enables us to attain that which we earnestly and diligently seek for.

THE

CÉNA UPANISHAD

OF THE

SAMA VÉDA.

1st. WHO is he [*asks a pupil of his spiritual father*] under whose sole will the intellectual power makes its approach *to different objects?* Who is he under whose authority *breath*, the primitive *power in the body*, makes its operation? Who is he by whose direction language is *regularly* pronounced? And who is that immaterial being that applies vision and hearing *to their respective objects?*

2d. He, [*answers the spiritual parent,*] who is the sense of the sense of hearing; the intellect of the intellect; the essential cause of language; the breath of breath; the sense of the sense of vision;—this is the being *concerning whom you would* enquire. Learned men having relinquished *the notion of self-independence. and self-consideration. from knowing the Supreme understanding to be the sole source of sense,* enjoy everlasting beatitude after their departure from this world.

3d. Hence no vision can approach him, no language can describe him, no intellectual power can compass or determine him. We know nothing of how the Supreme Being should be explained: he is beyond all that is within the reach of comprehension, and also beyond nature, which is above conception. Our ancient *spiritual parents* have thus explained him to us.

4th. He alone who has never been described by language, and who directs language *to its meaning*, is the Supreme Being, and not any specified thing which men worship: know THOU this.

5th. He alone whom understanding cannot comprehend, and who, as said *by learned men*, knows the real nature of understanding, is the Supreme Being, and not any specified thing which men worship: know THOU this.

6th. He alone whom no one can conceive by vision, and by whose superintendence every one perceives the objects of vision, is the Supreme Being, and not any specified thing which men worship: know THOU this.

7th. He alone whom no one can hear through the sense of hearing, and who knows the real nature of the sense of hearing, is the Supreme Being, and not any specified thing which men worship: know THOU this.

8th. He alone whom no one can perceive through the sense of smelling, and who applies the sense of smelling *to its objects*, is the Supreme Being, and not any specified thing which men worship: know THOU this.

9th. If you [*continues the spiritual parent*], *from what I have stated*, suppose *and say* that "I know the Supreme Being thoroughly," you in truth know very little of the Omnipresent Being; and any conception of that Being, which you limit to your powers of sense, is not only deficient, but also his description which you extend to *the* bodies of the celestial gods is also imperfect;* you consequently should enquire into the true knowledge of the Supreme Being. *To this the pupil replies:* "I perceive that *at this moment* I begin to know God."

10th. "Not that I suppose," *continues he,* "that I "know God thoroughly, nor do I suppose that I do "not know him at all; as, among us, he who knows the "meaning of the above-stated assertion is possessed "of the knowledge respecting God; *viz.* that I "neither know him thoroughly, nor am entirely igno- "rant of him."

11th. [*The Spiritual Father again resumes:*] He who believes that he cannot comprehend God *does* know him; and he who believes that he can comprehend God *does not* know him: as men of perfect understanding acknowledge him to be beyond comprehension; and men of imperfect understanding suppose him to be within the reach of their simplest perception.

12th. The notion of the sensibility of bodily organs, *which are composed of insensible particles,* leads to the notion of God; which notion alone is accurate, and tends to everlasting happiness. Man gains, by self exertion, the power of acquiring knowledge respecting God, and through the same acquisition he acquires eternal beatitude.

13th. Whatever person has, *according to the above stated doctrine,* known God, is really happy, and whoever

* The sum of the notion concerning the Supreme Being given in the Vedant, is, that he is "the soul of the universe;" and bears the same relation to all material extension that a human soul does to the individual body with which it is connected.

has not known him is subjected to great misery. Learned men, having reflected on the Spirit of God extending over all moveable as well as immoveable creatures, after their departure from this world are absorbed into the Supreme Being.

In a battle between the celestial gods and the demons,* God obtained victory over the latter, in favour of the former (*or properly speaking, God enabled the former to defeat the latter*); but, upon this victory being gained, the celestial gods acquired their respective dignities, and supposed that this victory and glory were entirely owing to themselves. The Omnipresent Being, having known their boast, appeared to them *with an appearance beyond description.*

They could not know what adorable appearance it was: they, *consequently,* said to fire, *or properly speaking the* god of fire: "Discover thou, O god of fire, what adorable appearance this is." His reply was, "I shall." He proceeded fast to that adorable appearance, which asked him, "Who art thou?" He then answered, "I "am fire, and I am the origin of the Véd;" *that is, I am a well-known personage.* The Supreme Omnipotence, upon being thus replied to, asked him *again,* "What "power is in so celebrated a person as thou art?" He replied, "I can burn to ashes all that exists in the "world." The Supreme Being then having laid a

* In the Ukhaika it is said that those powers of the Divinity, which produce agreeable effects and conduce to moral order and happiness, are represented under the figure of celestial Gods, and those attributes, from which pain and misery flow, are called Demons and step-brothers of the former, with whom they are in a state of perpetual hostility.

straw before him, said to him, "Canst thou burn this "straw?" The god of fire approached the straw, but could not burn it, though he exerted all his power: He then *unsuccessfully* retired and *told the others*, "I "have been unable to discover what adorable appear-"ance this is." Now they all said to wind (*or properly to the god of wind*), "Discover thou, O god of wind, "what adorable appearance this is." His reply was, "I shall." He proceeded fast to that adorable appearance, which asked him, "Who art thou?" He then answered, "I am wind, and I pervade unlimited "space;" *that is, I am a well-known personage.* The Supreme Being *upon being* thus replied to, asked him *again*, "What power is in so celebrated a person as "thou art?" He replied, "I can uphold all that exists "in the world." The Supreme Being then having laid a straw before him, said to him, "Canst thou up-"hold this straw?" The god of wind approached the straw, but could not hold it up, though he exerted all his power. He then *unsuccessfully* retired *and told the others*, "I have been unable to discover what ador-"able appearance this is." Now they all said to the god of atmosphere, "Discover thou, O revered god of "atmosphere, what adorable appearance this is." His reply was, "I shall." He proceeded fast to that adorable appearance, which vanished from his view. He met at the same spot a woman, *the goddess of instruction*, arrayed in golden robes in the shape of the most beautiful Uma.* He asked, "What was that adorable "appearance?" She replied, "It was the Supreme

* The wife of Siva.

"Being owing to whose victory you are all advanced "to exaltation." The god of atmosphere, from her instruction, knew that it was the Supreme Being *that had appeared to them. He at first communicated that information to the gods of fire and of wind.* As the gods of fire, wind, and atmosphere had approached to the adorable appearance, and had perceived it, and also as they had known, prior *to the others,* that it was indeed God *that appeared to them,* they seemed to be superior to the other gods. As the god of atmosphere had approached to the adorable appearance, and perceived it, and also as he knew, prior to *every one of them,* that it was God *that appeared to them,* he seemed not only superior to every other god, but also, *for that reason,* exalted above the gods of fire and wind.

The foregoing is a divine figurative representation of the Supreme Being; meaning that in one instant he shines at once *over all the universe* like the illumination of lightning; and in another, that he disappears as quick as the twinkling of an eye. Again it is represented *of the Supreme Being,* that *pure* mind conceives that it approaches to him as nearly as possible: Through the same pure mind the pious man thinks of him, and consequently application of the mind to him is repeatedly used. That God, *who alone in reality has no resemblance, and to whom the mind* cannot approach, is adorable by all living creatures; he is therefore called "*adorable*;" he should, *according to the prescribed manner*, be worshipped. All creatures revere the person who knows God in the manner thus described. The pupil *now says,* "Tell me, O Spiritual "Father, the Upanishad, or the principal part of the

"Véd." The *Spiritual Father makes this answer*, "I "have told you the principal part of the Véd, which "relates to God alone, and, indeed told you the Upani-"shad, of which, austere devotion, control over the "senses, performance of religious rites, and the remain-"ing parts of the Véd, as well as those sciences that "are derived from the Véds, are *only* the feet; and "whose altar and support is truth." He, who understands it as thus described, having relieved himself from sin, acquires eternal and unchangeable beatitude.

TRANSLATION

OF THE

KUT'H-OPUNISHUD

OF THE

UJOOR-VED,

ACCORDING TO THE GLOSS OF THE CELEBRATED

SUNKURACHARYU.

PREFACE.

In pursuance of my attempt to render a translation of the complete Vedant, or the principal parts of the Veds, into the current languages of this country, I had some time ago the satisfaction of publishing a translation of the Kut'h-opunishud of the Ujoor-ved into Bengalee; and of distributing copies of it as widely as my circumstances would allow, for the purpose of diffusing Hindoo Scriptural knowledge among the adherents of that religion. The present publication is intended to assist the European community in forming their opinion respecting Hindoo Theology, rather from the matter found in their doctrinal scriptures, than from the Poorans, moral tales, or any other modern works, or from the superstitious rites and habits daily encouraged and fostered by their self-interested leaders.

This work not only treats polytheism with contempt and disdain, but inculcates invariably the unity of God as the intellectual principle, the sole origin of individual intellect, entirely distinct from matter and its affections; and teaches also the mode of directing the mind to him.

A great body of my countrymen, possessed of good understandings, and not much fettered with prejudices, being perfectly satisfied with the truth of the doctrines contained in this and in other works, already laid by me before them, and of the gross errors of the peurile system of idol worship which they were led to follow, have altered their religious conduct in a manner becoming the dignity of human beings; while the advocates of idolatry and their misguided followers, over whose opinions prejudice and obstinacy prevail more than good sense and judgment, prefer custom and fashion to the authorities of their scriptures, and therefore continue, under the form of religious devotion, to practise a system which destroys, to the utmost degree, the natural texture of society, and prescribes crimes of the most heinous nature which even the most savage nations would blush to commit, unless compelled by the most urgent necessity.* I am, however, not without a sanguine hope that, through Divine Providence and human exertions, they will sooner or later avail themselves of that true system of religion which leads its observers to a knowledge and love of God, and to a friendly inclination towards their fellow-creatures, impressing their hearts at the same time with humility and charity, accompanied by independence of mind and pure sincerity. Contrary to the code of idolatry, this system defines sins as evil thoughts proceeding from the heart, quite unconnected with observances as to diet and other matters of form. At any rate, it seems to me that I cannot better employ my time than in an endeavour to illustrate and maintain truth, and to render service to my fellow-labourers, confiding in the mercy of that Being to whom the motives of our actions and secrets of our hearts are well known.

* Vide the latter end of the Introduction to the Moonduk Opunishud.

KUTH-OPUNISHUD.

DESIROUS *of future fruition,* Bajushrubusu *performed the sacrifice Vishwujit, at which* he distributed all his property. He had a son named Nuchiketa. *Old and infirm cows* being brought by the father as fees to be given to attending priests, the youth was seized with compassion, reflecting within himself, "He who gives "*to attending priests* such cows as are no longer able "to drink water or to eat grass, and are incapable of "giving further milk or of producing young, is carried "to that mansion where there is no felicity whatever."

He then said to his father, "To whom, O father, "wilt thou consign me over *in lieu of these cows?*" and repeated the same question a second and a third time.

Enraged with his presumption, the father replied to him, "I shall give thee to Yumu" *(the god of death). The youth then said to himself,* "*In the discharge of my* "*duties as a son,* I hold a foremost place among many "sons or pupils of the first class, and I am not inferior "to any of the sons or pupils of the second class: "whether my father had a previous engagement with "Yumu, which he will now perform by surrendering "me *to him, or made use of such an expression through* "*anger, I know not.*" *The youth finding his father afflicted with sorrow, said,* "Remember the meritorious

" conduct of our ancient *forefathers*, and observe the " virtuous acts of cotemporary good men. *Life is too* " *short to gain advantages by means of falsehood or breach* " *of promise;* as man like a plant is easily destroyed, " and again like it puts forth its form. *Do you there-* " *fore surrender me to Yumu according to your promise.*" *The youth Nuchiketa, by permission of his father, went to the habitation of Yumu. After he had remained there for three days without food or refreshment, Yumu returned to his dwelling, and was thus addressed by his family:* " A Brahmun entering a house as a guest is like fire; " *good householders, therefore,* extinguish his anger *by* " *offering him water, a seat, and food.* Do thou, O " Yumu! present him with water. A man deficient " in wisdom suffers his hopes, his sanguine expecta- " tions of success, his improvement from associating " with good men, the benefit which he might derive " from his affable conversation, and the fruits produced " by performance of prescribed sacrifices, and also by " digging of wells and other pious liberal actions, as " well as all his sons and cattle, to be destroyed, should " a Brahmun happen to remain in his house without " food."

Yumu being thus admonished by his family, approached Nuchiketa and said to him; " As thou, O Brahmun! " hast lived in my house, a revered guest, for the space " of three *days and* nights without food, I offer thee " reverence in atonement, so that bliss may attend me; " and do thou ask three favours *of me* as a recompense " for what thou hast suffered while dwelling in my house " during these three days past." *Nuchiketa then made this as his first request, saying,* " Let, O Yumu! my "father Gotum's apprehension *of my death* be removed, "his tranquillity of mind be restored, his anger against "me extinguished, and let him recognise me *on my re-* "*turn*, after having been set free by thee. This is the "first of three favours which I ask of thee." *Yumu then replied:*

"*Thy father*, styled Ouddaluki and Arooni, shall "have the same regard for you as before; so that, being "assured of thy existence, he shall, through my "power, repose the remaining nights *of his life* free "from sorrow, after having seen thee released from "the grasp of death." Nuchiketa then made his second request. "In heaven, where there is no fear "whatsoever, and where even thou, O Yumu! canst "not *always exercise thy authority*, and where, there- "fore, none dread *thy power, so much* as weak mortals "of the earth, the soul, unafflicted either by thirst "or hunger, and unmolested by sorrow, enjoys gra- "tification. As thou, O Yumu! dost possess know- "ledge respecting fire which is the means of attain- "ing heaven, do thou instruct me, who am full of "faith, in that knowledge; for, those who enjoy "heaven, owing to their observance of sacred fire, "are endowed with the nature of celestial deities. "This I ask of thee, as the second favour which "thou hast offered." *Yumu replied:* "Being pos- "sessed of a knowledge of fire, the means that lead to "the enjoyment of heavenly gratifications, I impart it "to thee; which do thou attentively observe. Know "thou fire, as means to obtain various mansions in "heaven, as the support *of the world*, and as residing "in the body."

Yumu explained to Nuchiketa the nature of fire, as being prior to all creatures, and also the particulars of the bricks and their number, which are requisite in forming the sacred fire, as well as the mode of preserving it. The youth repeated to Yumu these instructions exactly as imparted to him; at which Yumu being pleased, again spoke.

The liberal-minded Yumu, satisfied with Nuchiketa, thus says: "I shall bestow on thee another "favour, *which is*, that this sacred fire shall be styled "after thy name; and accept thou this valuable and "various-coloured necklace. Receiving instructions "from parents and spiritual fathers, a person who has "thrice collected fire, *as prescribed in the Ved*, and "also has been in habits of performing sacrifices, "studying the Veds, and giving alms, is not liable "to repeated birth and death: he, having known and "contemplated fire as originating from Bruhmá, possessing superior understanding, full of splendour, "and worthy of praise, enjoys the highest fruition. A "wise worshipper of sacred fire, who, understanding "the three things prescribed, has offered oblation "to fire, surmounting all afflictions during life, and "extricated from sorrow, will enjoy gratifications in "heaven.

"This, O Nuchiketa! is that knowledge of sacred "fire, the means of obtaining heaven, which thou "didst require of me as the second favour; men shall "call it after thy name. Make, O Nuchiketa! thy "third request."

Nuchiketa then said: "Some are of opinion that "after man's demise existence continues, and others

“ say it ceases. Hence a doubt has arisen *respecting* “ *the nature of the soul;* I therefore wish to be in- “ structed by thee in this matter. This is the last “ of the favours thou hast offered.” *Yumu replied:* “ Even gods have doubted and disputed on this sub- “ ject; which being obscure, never can be thorough- “ ly comprehended: Ask, O Nuchiketa! another “ favour *instead of this.* Do not thou take advan- “ tage of my promise, but give up this request.” *Nuchiketa replied:* “ *I am* positively informed that “ Gods entertained doubts on this subject; and even “ thou, O Yumu! callest it difficult of comprehen- “ sion. But no instructor on this point equal to “ thee can be found, and no other object is so desir- “ able as this.” Yumu said: “ Do thou rather request “ of me to give thee sons and grandsons, each to “ attain the age of an hundred years; numbers of “ cattle, elephants, gold, and horses; also extensive “ empire on earth, where thou shalt live as many “ years as thou wishest.

“ If thou knowest another object equally desirable “ with these, ask it; together with wealth and long “ life. Thou mayest reign, O Nuchiketa! over a “ great kingdom: I will enable thee to enjoy all “ wished-for objects.

“ Ask according to thy desire all objects that are “ difficult of acquisition in the mortal world. Ask “ these beautiful women, with elegant equipages and “ musical instruments, as no man can acquire any “ thing like them *without our gift.* Enjoy thou “ the attendance of these women, whom I may “ bestow on thee; but do not put to me, O Nu-

"chiketa! the question respecting existence after "death."

Nuchiketa then replied. "The acquisition of the "enjoyments thou hast offered, O Yumu! is *in the* "*first place* doubtful; and should they be obtained, "they destroy the strength of all the senses; and even "the life of Bruhmá is, indeed, comparatively short. "Therefore let thy equipages, and thy dancing and "music, remain with thee.

"No man can be satisfied with riches; and as we "have *fortunately* beheld thee, we may acquire wealth, "should we feel desirous of it; and we also may live "as long as thou exercisest the authority of the god "of death; but the only object I desire is what I have "already begged *of thee.*

"A mortal being, whose habitation is the low man-"sion of earth, and who is liable to sudden reduction, "approaching the gods exempted from death and "debility, and understanding from them *that there is a* "*knowledge of futurity, should not ask of them any infe-*"*rior favour*—and knowing the fleeting nature of "music, sexual gratification, and sensual pleasures, "who can take delight in a long life on earth? Do "thou instruct us in that knowledge which removes "doubts respecting existence after death, and is of "great importance with a view to futurity, and which "is obscure and acquirable with difficulty. I, Nuchi-"keta, cannot ask any other favour but this."

End of the first Section of the first Chapter.

Yumu now, after a sufficient trial of Nuchiketa's resolution, answers the third question, saying, "Knowledge

" of God which leads to absorption, is one thing; and " rites, which have fruition for their object, another: " each of these producing different consequences, holds " out to man inducements to follow it. The man, " who of these two chooses knowledge, is blessed; and " he who, *for the sake of reward*, practises rites, is " excluded from the enjoyment of eternal beatitude. " Knowledge and rites both offer themselves to man; " but he who is possessed of wisdom, taking their " respective natures into serious consideration, dis- " tinguishes one from the other, and chooses faith, " despising fruition; and a fool, for the sake of ad- " vantage and enjoyment, accepts the offer of rites.

" Thou, O Nuchiketa! knowing the perishable na- " ture of the desirable and gratifying objects offered " by me, hast rejected them, and refused the adoption " of that contemptible practice, which leads to frui- " tion and to riches, and to which men in general are " attached. Wise men *are sensible* that a knowledge " of God, *which procures absorption*, and the perform- " ance of rites *that produces fruition*, are entirely oppo- " site to each other, and yield different consequences. " I conceive thee, Nuchiketa, to be desirous of a " knowledge of God; for the numerous estimable ob- " jects offered by me cannot tempt thee. Surrounded " by the darkness of ignorance, fools consider them- " selves wise and learned, and wander about in va- " rious directions, like blind men when guided by a " blind man."

To an indiscreet man who lives carelessly, and is immersed in the desire of wealth, the means of gaining heavenly beatitude are not manifest. He thinks that this visible world alone exists, and that there is nothing hereafter; consequently he is repeatedly subjected to my control. The soul is that of whose real nature many persons have never heard; and several though they have heard, have not comprehended. A man who is capable of giving instruction on this subject is rare: One who listens to it attentively, must be intelligent: and that one who, being taught by a wise teacher, understands it, is uncommon.

If a man of inferior abilities describe the nature of the soul, no one will thoroughly understand it; for various opinions are held *by contending parties.* When the subject is explained by a person who believes the soul to emanate from God, doubt, in regard to its eternity, ceases; but otherwise it is inexplicable and not capable of demonstration.

The knowledge respecting the soul which thou wilt gain by me, cannot be acquired by means of reason alone; but it should be obtained from him who is versed in the sacred authorities. Oh, beloved pupil, Nuchiketa! may we have enquirers like thee, who art full of resolution. I know that fruition, acquirable by means of rites, is perishable; for nothing eternal can be obtained through perishable means. *Notwithstanding my conviction of the destructible nature of fruition,* I performed the worship of the sacred fire, whereby I became possessed of this sovereignty of long duration.

Thou, Oh wise Nuchiketa! hast through firmness refused, though offered to thee, the state of Bruhmá; which satisfies every desire, and which is the support of the world—the best consequence of the performance of rites without limit or fear—praiseworthy—full of superhuman power—extensive and stable.

The soul is that which is difficult to be comprehended—most obscure—veiled by the ideas acquired through the senses, and which resides in faculties—does not depart even in great danger, and exists unchangeable. A wise man knowing the resplendent soul, through a mind abstracted from worldly objects, and constantly applied to it, neither rejoices nor does he grieve.

A mortal who, having heard the pure doctrines relative to the soul and retained them in his memory, knowing the invisible soul to be distinct from *the body*, feels rejoiced at his acquisition. I think the abode of the knowledge of God is open to thee.

Nuchiketa then asked, "If thou knowest any Being "who *exists* distinctly from rites, their consequences "and their observers, and also from evil, and who "is different from effects and their respective causes, "and is above past, future, and present time, do "thou inform me."

Yumu replies: "I will explain to thee briefly that "Being whom all the Veds treat of, *either directly or* "*indirectly*, to whom all austerities are directed, and "who is the main object of those who perform the "duties of an ascetic, He, to wit, whom the word "Om implies, is the Supreme Being."

That Om is the title of Bruhmá and also of the Supreme Being, through means of which man may gain what he wishes; *(that is, if he worship Bruhmá by means of Om, he shall be received into his mansion; or if through it he elevate his mind to God, he shall obtain absorption.)*

Om is the best of all means *calculated* to direct the mind towards God; and it is instrumental either in the acquisition of the knowledge of God *or of the dignity of Bruhmá:* man therefore having recourse to this word, shall either be absorbed in God, or revered like Bruhmá.

The soul is not liable to birth nor to death: it is mere understanding: neither does it take its origin from any other or from itself: hence it is unborn, eternal without reduction and unchangeable; therefore the soul is not injured by the hurt which the body may receive. If any one ready to kill another imagine that he can destroy his soul, and the other think that his soul shall suffer destruction, they both know nothing; for neither does it kill nor is it killed by *another.*

The soul is the smallest of the small, and greatest of the great. It resides in the hearts of all living creatures. A man who knows it and its pure state, through the steadiness of the external and internal senses, acquired from the abandoning of worldly desires, overcomes sorrow and perplexity.

The soul, although without motion, seems to go to furthest space; and though it resides in the body at rest, yet seems to move every where. Who can perceive besides myself, that splendid soul, the support of the sensations of happiness and pain?

The soul, although it is immaterial, yet resides closely attached to perishable material objects: knowing it as great and extensive, a wise man never grieves for it. A knowledge of the soul is not acquirable from the study of the Veds, nor through retentive memory, nor yet by constant hearing of spiritual instruction: but he who seeks to obtain a knowledge of it, is gifted with it; the soul rendering itself conspicuous to him.

No man can acquire a knowledge of the soul without abstaining from evil acts; without having control over the senses and the mind; nor can he gain it with a mind, though firm, yet filled with the desire of fruition; but man may obtain a knowledge of the soul through his knowledge of God.

No *ignorant* man can, in a perfect manner, know the state of the existence of that God whose food is *all things*, even the Brahmun and the Kshutri; *(that is, who destroys every object bearing figure and appellation)*; and who consumes death itself even as butter.

The end of the second section of the first chapter.

God and the soul entering into the heart, the excellent divine abode, consume, while residing in the body, the necessary consequences of its actions; *that is, the latter is rewarded or punished according to its good or evil actions, and the former witnesses all those events.* Those who have a knowledge of God, consider the former as light and the latter as shade: the observers of external rites also, as well as those who have collected fire three times for worship, believe the same.

We can *know and collect fire*, which is a bridge to the observers of rites; and can know the eternal and fearless God, who is the conveyer of those who wish to cross the ocean of ignorance. Consider the soul as a rider, the body as a car, the intellect its driver, the mind as its rein: the external senses are called the horses, restrained by the mind; external objects are the roads: so wise men believe the soul united with the body, the senses and the mind, to be the partaker *of the consequences of good or evil acts.*

If that intellect, *which is represented as the driver,* be indiscreet, and the rein of the mind loose, all the senses *under the authority of the intellectual power* become unmanageable; like wicked horses under the control of an *unfit* driver.

If the intellect be discreet and the rein of the mind firm, all the senses prove steady and manageable; like good horses under an excellent driver.

He, who has not a prudent intellect and steady mind, and who consequently lives always impure, cannot arrive at the divine glory, but descends to the world.

He who has a prudent intellect and steady mind, and consequently lives always pure, attains that glory from whence he never will descend.

Man who has intellect as his prudent driver, and a steady mind as his rein, passing over the paths of mortality, arrives at the high glory of the omnipresent God.

The origin of the senses is more refined than the senses; the essence of the mind is yet more refined than that origin: the source of intellect is again more exalted than that of the mind; the prime sensitive particle is superior to the source of intellect; nature, the apparent cause of the universe, is again superior to that particle, to which the omnipresent God is still superior: nothing is more exalted than God: he is therefore superior to all existences, and is the Supreme object of all. God exists obscurely throughout the universe, *consequently* is not perceived; but he is known through the acute intellect constantly directed towards him by wise men of penetrating understandings. A wise man shall transfer the power of speech and that of the senses to the mind, and the mind to the intellect, and the intellect to the *purified* soul, and the soul to the unchangeable Supreme Being.

Rise up and awake *from the sleep of ignorance;* and having approached able teachers, acquire knowledge *of God, the origin of the soul:* for the way to the knowledge of God is considered by wise men difficult as the passage over the sharp edge of a razor. The Supreme Being is not organised with the faculties of hearing, feeling, vision, taste or smell. He is unchangeable and eternal; without beginning or end; and is beyond that particle which is the origin of the intellect: *man* knowing him thus, is relieved from the grasp of death.

A wise man reading to *Brahmuns*, or hearing *from a teacher*, this ancient doctrine imparted to Nuchiketa by Yumu, is absorbed into God.

He who reads this most secret doctrine before an assemblage of Brahmuns, or at the time of offering oblations to his forefathers, enjoys innumerable good consequences.

The end of the third Bullee.

God has created the senses to be directed towards external objects; they consequently are apt to perceive outward things only, and not the eternal spirit. But a wise man being desirous of eternal life, withdrawing his senses from their natural course, apprehends the omnipresent Supreme Being.

The ignorant seek external and desirable objects only; *consequently* they are subjected to the chain of all-seizing death. Hence the wise, knowing that God alone is immortal and eternal in this perishable world, do not cherish a wish *for those objects.*

To him, owing to whose presence alone the animate beings, *composed of insensible particles,* perceive objects through vision, the power of taste, of feeling, and of hearing, and also the pleasure derivable from sexual intercourse, nothing can be unknown: he is that existence which *thou desiredst to know.*

A wise man after having known that the soul, owing to whose presence living creatures perceive objects, whether they dream or wake, is great and extensive, never grieves.

He who believes that the soul, which enjoys the fruits of good or evil actions, intimately connected with the body, originates from and is united with God, the Lord of past and future events, will not conceal its nature: he is that existence which thou desiredst to know. He who knows that the prime sensitive particle, which proceeded from God prior to the creation of water and the other elements, having entered into the heart, exists united with material objects, knows the Supreme Being. He is that existence which thou desiredst to know.

That sensitive particle which perceives objects, and includes all the celestial deities, and which was created with all the elements, exists, entering into the space of the heart, and there resides. It is that existence which thou desiredst to know.

The sacred fire, the receiver of oblations, after the wood has been kindled below and above, is preserved by its observers with the same care as pregnant women take of their fœtus: it is praised daily by prudent observers, and men habituated to constant devotion. That atmosphere from whence the sun ascends, and in which he goes down, on which all the world, *including fire, speech, and other* things, rests, and independently of which nothing exists, is that existence which thou desiredst to know. Whatever individual intellect there is connected with the body, is that intellectual principle, which is pure and immaterial existence, and the intellectual overspreading principle is the individual intellect; but he who thinks here that they are different in nature, is subject to repeated transmigrations.

Through the mind, *purified by spiritual instructions,* the knowledge that the soul is of divine origin, and by no means is different *from its source,* shall be acquired, whereby the idea of duality entirely ceases. He who thinks there is variety of intellectual principle, undergoes transmigration.

The omnipresent spirit, extending over the space of the heart, which is the size of a finger, resides within the body; and persons knowing him the Lord of past and future events, will not again attempt to conceal his nature: He is that existence which thou desiredst to know.

The omnipresent spirit which extends over the space of the heart, the size of a finger, is the most pure light. He is the Lord of past and future events; He alone pervades *the universe* now and ever; He is that existence which thou desiredst to know. In the same way as water falling on uneven ground disperses throughout the hollow places, and is lost, so a man who thinks that the souls of different bodies are distinct in nature from each other, shall be placed in various forms by transmigration.

As water falling on even grounds remains unchanged, so the soul of a wise man of steady mind is *always* pure, freed from the idea of duality.

End of the fourth Bullee.

The body is a dwelling with eleven gates, belonging to the unborn and unchangeable spirit, through whose constant contemplation man escapes from grief, and acquiring absorption, is exempted from transmigration. He is that existence which thou desiredst to know.

That spiritual Being acts *always* and moves in heaven; preserves all material existence as depending on him; moves in space; resides in fire; walks on the earth; enters like a guest into sacrificial vessels; dwells in man, in gods, in sacrifices; moves throughout the sky; seems to be born in water, *as fishes, &c.;* produced on earth, *as vegetables,* on the tops of mountains, *as rivers,* and also as members of sacrifices: yet is he truly pure and great. He who causes breath to ascend above the heart and peditum to descend, resides in the heart: He is adorable; and to him all the senses offer oblation of the objects which they perceive.

When the soul, which is connected with the body, leaves it, nothing then remains in the body which may preserve the system: It is that existence which thou desiredst to know.

Neither by the help of breath, nor from the presence of other powers, can a mortal exist: but they all exist owing to that other existence on which both breath and the senses rest.

I will now disclose to you the secret doctrine of the eternal God; and also how man, *void of that knowledge*, O Goutum! transmigrates after death.

Some of those *who are ignorant of this doctrine* enter after death the womb of females to appear in the animal shape, while others assume the form of trees, according to their conduct and knowledge *during their lives.*

The Being who continues to operate even at that time of sleep, when all the senses cease to act, and then creates desirable objects of various descriptions, is pure and the greatest of all; and he alone is called eternal, on whom all the world rests, and independently of whom nothing can exist: He is that existence which thou desiredst to know. As fire, although one in essence, on becoming visible in the world, appears in various forms and shapes, according to its different locations, so God, the soul of the universe, though one, appears in various modes, according as he connects himself with different material objects, and, *like space*, extends over all.

As air, although one in essence, in becoming operative in the body appears in various natures, as breath and other vital airs, so God, the soul of the universe, though one, appears in different modes, according as he connects himself with various material objects, and, *like space*, extends over all.

As the sun, though he serves as the eye of all living

creatures, yet is not polluted externally *or internally* by being connected with visible vile objects, so God, the soul of the universe, although one and omnipresent, is not affected by the sensations of individual pain, for he is beyond its action.

God is but one; and he has the whole world under his control, for he is the operating soul in all objects: He, *through his omniscience,* makes his sole existence appear in the form of the universe. To those wise men who acquire a knowledge of him who is operative on the human faculties, is eternal beatitude allotted, and not to those who are void of that knowledge.

God is eternal amidst the perishable universe; and is the source of sensation among all animate existences; and he alone assigns to so many objects their respective purposes: To those wise men who know him the ruler of the intellectual power, everlasting beatitude is allotted; but not to those who are void of that knowledge.

How can I acquire that most gratifying divine knowledge, which, though beyond comprehension, *wise men, by constant application of mind, alone obtain,* as if it were present? Does it shine conspicuously?—and does it appear to the human faculties?

Neither the sun, nor the moon, nor yet the stars can throw light on God: Even the illuminating lightning cannot throw light upon him; much less can limited fire give him light: But they all imitate him, and all borrow their light from him—*that is, nothing can influence God and render him perspicuous: But God himself imparts his knowledge to the heart freed from passion and desire.*

End of the fifth Bullee.

The world is a fig-tree of long duration, whose origin is above, and the branches of which, *as different species*, are below. The origin alone is pure and supreme; and he alone is eternal on whom all the world rests, and independently of whom nothing can exist.—He is that existence which thou desiredst to know.

God being eternal existence, the universe, whatsoever it is, exists and proceeds from him. He is the great dread of all *heavenly bodies*, as if he were prepared to strike them with thunderbolts; *so that none of them can deviate from their respective courses established by him.* Those who know him as the eternal power acquire absorption.

Through his fear fire supplies *us* with heat; and the sun, through his fear, shines *regularly;* and also Indru, and air, and fifthly, death, are through his fear constantly in motion.

If *man* can acquire a knowledge of God in this world, before the fall of his body, *he becomes happy for ever:* Otherwise he assumes new forms in different mansions. *A knowledge of God shines* on the purified intellect in this world, as clearly as an object is seen by reflection in a polished mirror: In the region of the deified Progenitors of mankind *it is viewed* as obscurely as objects perceived in the state of dreaming; and in the mansion of Gundhurvus, in the same degree as the reflection of an object on water; but in the mansion of Bruhmá it appears as distinctly as the difference between light and darkness.

A wise man, knowing the soul to be distinct from the senses, which proceed from different origins, and also from the state of waking and of sleep, never again grieves.

The mind is more refined than the external senses; and the intellect is again more exalted than the mind. The prime sensitive particle is superior to the intellect; —nature, the apparent cause of the universe, is again superior to that particle unaffected by matter: *Superior to nature is God*, who is omnipresent and without material effects: by acquisition of whose knowledge man becomes extricated from ignorance and distress, and is absorbed into Him *after death*. His substance does not come within the reach of vision; no one can apprehend him through the senses: By constant direction of the intellect, free from doubts, he perspicuously appears; and those who know him in the prescribed manner, enjoy eternal life.

That part of life wherein the power of the five external senses and the mind are directed towards the Supreme Spirit, and the intellectual power ceases its action, is said to be most sacred; and this steady control of the senses and mind is considered to be *Yog (or withdrawing the senses and the mind from worldly objects)*: Man should be vigilant in the acquisition of that state; for such control proceeds from constant exercise, and ceases by neglect.

Neither through speech, nor through intellectual power, nor yet through vision, can man acquire a knowledge of God; but, save him who believes in the existence of God *as the cause of the universe*, no one can have a notion of that Being. A man should acquire, first, a belief in the existence of God, the origin of the universe; and next, a real knowledge of him; to wit, that he is incomprehensible; for the means which lead men to acquire a knowledge of his existence, graciously conduct them to the belief of his incomprehensibility. When all the desires settled in the heart leave man, the mortal then become immortal, and acquire absorption even in this life. When the deep ignorance *which occasions duality* is entirely destroyed, the mortal become immortal: This is the only doctrine which *the Vedant* inculcates.

There are one hundred and one tubes connected with the heart, one of *which, called Sookhumna,* proceeds to the head: The soul of a devotee proceeding through the hundred and first, is carried to the mansion of the immortal Bruhmá; and those of others, which ascend by other tubes, assume different bodies, *according to the evil or good acts which they perform.*

The omnipresent eternal spirit resides always within that space of the human heart which is as large as a finger: Man should, by firmness of mind, separate that spirit from the body, in the same manner as the pith is removed from the plant Moonju: *that is, the spirit should be considered totally distinct from matter and the effects of matter*—and man should know that separated spirit to be pure and eternal.

Having thus acquired this divine doctrine, imparted by the God of death, with every thing belonging to it, Nuchiketa, freed from the consequences of good or evil acts, and from mortality, was absorbed into God: and whatever person also can acquire that knowledge, shall obtain absorption.

End of the Kut'h-opunishud.

TRANSLATION

OF THE

ISHOPANISHAD,

One of the chapters of the

YAJUR VÉDA:

ACCORDING TO THE COMMENTARY OF THE CELEBRATED

SHANKAR - ÁCHÁRYA:

ESTABLISHING THE UNITY AND INCOMPREHENSIBILITY OF

THE SUPREME BEING;

AND THAT

HIS WORSHIP ALONE

CAN LEAD TO ETERNAL BEATITUDE.

CALCUTTA:
1816.

PREFACE.

THE most learned Vyasa shows, in his work of the Védánt, that all the texts of the Véd, with one consent, prove but the Divinity of that Being, who is out of the reach of comprehension and beyond all description. For the use of the public, I have made a concise translation of that celebrated work into Bengalee, and the present is an endeavour to translate* the principal Chapters of the Véd, in conformity to the Comments of the great Shankar-Acharya. The translation of the Ishopanishad belonging to the Yajur, the second division of the Védas, being already completed, I have put it into the press;† and the others will successively be printed, as soon as their translation is completed. It is evident, from those authorities, that the sole regulator of the Universe is but one, who is omnipresent, far surpassing our powers of comprehension; above external sense; and whose worship is the chief duty of mankind and the sole cause of eternal beatitude; and that all that bear figure and appellation are inven-

* I must confess how much I feel indebted to Doctor H. H. Wilson, in my translations from Sunskrit into English, for the use of his Sunskrit and English Dictionary.

† Wherever any comment, upon which the sense of the original depends, is added to the original, it will be found written in Italics.

tions. Should it be asked, whether the assertions found in the Puranas* and Tantras, &c. respecting the worship of the several gods and goddesses, are false, or whether Puranas and Tantras are not included in the Shastra, the answer is this:—The Purana and Tantra,† &c. are of course to be considered as Shastra, for they repeatedly declare God to be one and above the apprehension of external and internal senses; they indeed expressly declare the divinity of many gods and goddesses, and the modes of their worship; but they reconcile those contradictory assertions by affirming frequently, that the directions to worship any figured beings are only applicable to those, who are incapable of elevating their minds to the idea of an invisible Supreme Being, in order that such persons, by fixing their attention on those invented figures, may be able to restrain themselves from vicious temptations, and that those that are competent for the worship of the invisible God, should disregard the worship of Idols. I repeat a few of these declarations as follows. The authority of Jamadagni is thus quoted by the great Raghunandan: "For the benefit of those "who are inclined to worship, figures are invented to "serve as representations of God, who is merely un-"derstanding, and has no second, no parts nor figure; "consequently, to these representatives, either male or "female forms and other circumstances are fictitiously "assigned." In the second Chapter of the first part of the Vishnu Purana it is said; "God is without "figure, epithet, definition or description. He is

* Said to have been written by Vyas.

† Supposed to have been composed by Shiva.

"without defect, not liable to annihilation, change, "pain or birth; we can only say, That he, who is the "eternal being, is God."—"The vulgar look for their "gods in water; men of more extended knowledge "in celestial bodies; the ignorant in wood, bricks, "and stones; but learned men in the universal soul." —In the 84th Chapter of the tenth division of the Sri Bhagavat, Crishna says to Vyas and others: "It is "impossible for those who consider pilgrimage as "devotion, and believe that the divine nature exists "in the image, to look up to, communicate with, to "petition and to revere true believers in God. He who "views as the soul this body formed of phlegm, wind and "bile, or regards only wife, children, and relations as "himself (that is, he who neglects to contemplate the "nature of the soul), he who attributes a divine nature "to earthern images, and believes in the holiness of "water, yet pays not such respect to those who are "endowed with a knowledge of God, is as an ass amongst "cows."

In the 9th Chapter of the Cularnava it is written: "A knowledge of the Supreme Being, who is beyond "the power of expression and unchangeable, being "acquired, all gods and goddesses, and their texts "which represent them, shall become slaves."—"After "a knowledge of the Supreme Being has been attained, "there is no need to attend to ceremonies prescribed "by Shastras—no want of a fan should be felt, when "a soft southern wind is found to refresh."—The Mahanirvana says, "Thus corresponding to the na-"tures of different powers or qualities, numerous "figures have been invented for the benefit of those

" who are not possessed of sufficient understanding."— From the foregoing quotations it is evident, that though the Véds, Puranas, and Tantras, frequently assert the existence of the plurality of gods and goddesses, and prescribe the modes of their worship for men of insufficient understanding, yet they have also declared in a hundred other places, that these passages are to be taken merely in a figurative sense.

It cannot be alleged in support of Idolatry, that " although a knowledge of God is certainly above all " things, still as it is impossible to acquire that know- " ledge, men should of course worship figured Gods ;" for, had it been impossible to attain a knowledge of the Supreme Being, the Véds and Purans, as well as Tantras, would not have instructed mankind to aim at such attainment; as it is not to be supposed that directions to acquire what is obviously unattainable could be given by the Shastra, or even by a man of common sense. Should the Idolater say, " that the acquisition " of a knowledge of God, although it is not impossible, " is most difficult of comprehension," I will agree with him in that point; but infer from it, that we ought, therefore, the more to exert ourselves to acquire that knowledge ; but I highly lament to observe, that so far from endeavouring to make such an acquisition, the very proposal frequently excites his anger and displeasure.

Neither can it be alleged that the Véds, Puranas, &c. teach both the adoration of the Supreme Being and that of celestial gods and goddesses, but that the former is intended for Yatis, or those that are bound by their profession to forsake all worldly considerations, and the latter for Laymen; for, it is evident from the 48th Text of the 3d Chapter of the Vedánt, that a householder also is required to perform the worship of the Supreme Being.

Menu, also, the chief of Hindoo lawgivers, after having prescribed all the varieties of rites and ceremonies, in Chapter 12th, Text 92, says, "Thus must the chief "of the twice-born, though he neglect the ceremonial "rites mentioned in the Shastras, be diligent in attaining a knowledge of God, in controlling his organs of "sense, and in repeating the Véd."

Again in the 4th Chapter, in describing the duties of Laymen, the same author says, "Some, who well know "the ordinances for the oblations, do not perform externally the five great sacraments, but continually "make offerings in their own organs *of sensation and* "*intellect.*"

"Some constantly sacrifice their breath in their "speech, *when they instruct others of God aloud,* and "their speech in their breath, *when they meditate in* "*silence,* perceiving in their speech and breath thus "employed the imperishable fruit of a sacrificial offering."

"Other Brahmins incessantly perform those sacrifices only, seeing with the eye of divine learning, that "the scriptural knowledge is the root of every ceremonial observance."

IN THE YAGNYAVALCA IT IS WRITTEN.

"Even a householder, who acquires a livelihood "honestly, has faith in the Supreme Being, shows hospitality to his guests, performs sacramental rites to "his forefathers, and is in the practice of telling truth, "shall be absorbed into the supreme essence." Should it be said, "It still remains unaccountable, that notwithstanding the Véds and Purans repeatedly declare "the unity of the Supreme Being, and direct mankind "to adore him alone, yet the generality of Hindoos "have a contrary faith, and continue to practise idolatry," I would in answer request attention to the foundation on which the practical part of the Hindoo religion is built. Many learned Brahmins are perfectly aware of the absurdity of idolatry, and are well informed of the nature of the purer mode of divine worship. But as in the rites, ceremonies, and festivals of idolatry, they find the source of their comforts and fortune, they not only never fail to protect idol worship from all attacks, but even advance and encourage it to the utmost of their power, by keeping the knowledge of their scriptures concealed from the rest of the people. Their followers too, confiding in these leaders, feel gratification in the idea of the Divine Nature residing in a being resembling themselves in birth, shape, and propensities; and are naturally delighted with a mode of worship agreeable to the senses, though destructive of moral principles, and the fruitful parent of prejudice and superstition.

Some Europeans, indued with high principles of liberality, but unacquainted with the ritual part of Hindoo idolatry, are disposed to palliate it by an interpretation which, though plausible, is by no means well founded. They are willing to imagine, that the idols which the Hindoos worship, are not viewed by them in the light of gods or as real personifications of the divine attributes, but merely as instruments for raising their minds to the contemplation of those attributes, which are respectively represented by different figures. I have frequently had occasion to remark, that many Hindoos also who are conversant with the English language, finding this interpretation a more plausible apology for idolatry than any with which they are furnished by their own guides, do not fail to avail themselves of it, though in repugnance both to their faith and to their practice. The declarations of this description of Hindoos naturally tend to confirm the original idea of such Europeans, who from the extreme absurdity of pure unqualified idolatry, deduce an argument against its existence. It appears to them impossible for men, even in the very last degree of intellectual darkness, to be so far misled as to consider a mere image of wood or of stone as a *human being*, much less as a divine existence. With a view, therefore, to do away any misconception of this nature which may have prevailed, I beg leave to submit the following considerations.

Hindoos of the present age, with a very few exceptions, have not the least idea that it is to the attributes of the Supreme Being, as figuratively represented by shapes corresponding to the nature of those attributes, they offer adoration and worship under the denomination of gods and goddesses. On the contrary, the slightest investigation will clearly satisfy every inquirer, that it makes a material part of their system to hold as articles of faith all those particular circumstances, which are essential to a belief in the independent existence of the objects of their idolatry as deities clothed with divine power.

Locality of habitation and a mode of existence analogous to their own views of earthly things, are uniformly ascribed to each particular god. Thus the devotees of Siva, misconceiving the real spirit of the Scriptures, not only place an implicit credence in the separate existence of Siva, but even regard him as an omnipotent being, the greatest of all the divinities, who, as they say, inhabit the northern mountain of Cailas; and that he is accompanied by two wives and several children, and surrounded with numerous attendants. In like manner the followers of Vishnu, mistaking the allegorical representations of the Sastras for relations of real facts, believe him to be chief over all other gods, and that he resides with his wife and attendants on the summit of heaven. Similar opinions are also held by the worshippers of Cali, in respect to that goddess. And in fact, the same observations are equally applicable to every class of Hindoo devotees in regard to their respective gods and goddesses. And so tenacious are those devotees in respect to the honour due to their chosen divinities, that when they meet in such holy places as Haridwar, Pryag, Siva-Canchi, or Vishnu-Canchi in the Dekhin, the adjustment of the point of precedence not only occasions the warmest verbal altercations, but sometimes even blows and violence. Neither do they regard the images of those gods merely in the light of instruments for elevating the mind to the conception of those supposed beings; they are simply in themselves made objects of worship. For whatever Hindoo purchases an idol in the market, or constructs one with his own hands, or has one made up under his own superintendence, it is his invariable practice to perform certain ceremonies, called Prán

Pratisht'ha, or the endowment of animation; by which he believes that its nature is changed from that of the mere materials of which it is formed, and that it acquires not only life but supernatural powers. Shortly afterwards, if the idol be of the masculine gender, he marries it to a feminine one, with no less pomp and magnificence than he celebrates the nuptials of his own children. The mysterious process is now complete, and the god and goddess are esteemed the arbiters of his destiny, and continually receive his most ardent adoration.

At the same time, the worshipper of images ascribes to them at once the opposite natures of human and of super-human beings. In attention to their supposed wants as living beings, he is seen feeding, or pretending to feed them every morning and evening; and as in the hot season he is careful to fan them, so in the cold he is equally regardful of their comfort, covering them by day with warm clothing, and placing them at night in a snug bed. But superstition does not find a limit here: the acts and speeches of the idols, and their assumption of various shapes and colours, are gravely related by the Brahmins, and with all the marks of veneration are firmly believed by their deluded followers. Other practices they have with regard to those idols which decency forbids me to explain. In thus endeavouring to remove a mistake, into which I have reason to believe many European gentlemen have been led by a benevolent wish to find an excuse for the errors of my countrymen, it is a considerable gratification to me to find that the latter have begun to be so far sensible of the absurdity of their real belief and practices, as to find it convenient to shelter them under such a cloak, however flimsy and borrowed. The adoption of such a subterfuge encourages me greatly to hope, that they will in time abandon what they are sensible cannot be defended; and that, forsaking the superstition of idolatry, they will embrace the rational worship of the God of Nature, as enjoined by the Véds, and confirmed by the dictates of common sense.

The argument which is frequently alleged in support of idolatry is, that "those who believe God to "be omnipresent, as declared by the doctrines of the "Védánt, are required by the tenets of such belief "to look upon all existing creatures as God, and to "shew divine respect to birds, beasts, men, women, ve-"getables, and all other existences; and as practical "conformity to such doctrines is almost impossible, the "worship of figured gods should be admitted." This misrepresentation, I am sorry to observe, entirely serves the purpose intended, by frightening Hindoos in general from attending to the pure worship of the Supreme Regulator of the universe. But I am confident that the least reflection on the subject will clear up this point beyond all doubt; for the Védánt is well known as a work which inculcates only the unity of God; but if every existing creature should be taken for a god by the followers of the Védánt, the doctrines of that work must be admitted to be much more at variance with that idea than those of the advocates of idolatry, as the latter are contented with the recognition of only a few millions of gods and goddesses, but the Védánt in that case must be supposed to admit the divinity of every living creature in nature. The fact is, that the Védánt, by declaring that "God is every "where, and every thing is in God," means that nothing is absent from God, and nothing bears real existence except by the volition of God, whose existence is the sole support of the conceived existence of the universe, which is acted upon by him in the same manner as a human body is by a soul. But God is at the same time quite different from what we see or feel.

The following texts of the Védánt are to this effect (11th text of the 2d section of the 3d chapter of the Vedant): "That being, which is distinct from matter, "and from those which are contained in matter, is not "various, because he is declared by all the Véds to be "one beyond description;" and again, "The Véd has "declared the Supreme Being to be mere understand-"ing." Moreover, if we look at the conduct of the ancient true believers in God, as Janaca, the celebrated prince of Mithila, Vasisht'ha, Sanaca, Vyasa, Sancaracharyu, and others whose characters as believers in one God are well known to the public by their doctrines and works, which are still in circulation, we shall find that these teachers, although they declared their faith in the omnipresent God according to the doctrines of the Védánt, assigned to every creature the particular character and respect he was entitled to. It is, however, extremely remarkable, that the very argument which they employ to shew the impossibility of practical conformity to faith in the omnipresence of God, may be alleged against every system of their own idolatry; for the believers in the godhead of Crishna, and the devotees of Cali, as well as the followers of Siva, believe firmly in the omnipresence of Crishna,* Cali,† and Siva,‡ respectively. The authorities, then, for the worship of those gods, in declaring their omnipresence, would according to their own argument, enjoin the worship of every creature as much as of those supposed divinities. Omnipresence, however, is an attribute much more consonant with the idea of a Supreme Being than with that of any fictitious figure to which they pay divine honours! Another argument is, that "No man "can have, as it is said by the Sastra, a desire of "knowledge respecting the Supreme Being, unless his "mind be purified; and as idol worship purifies men's "minds, it should be therefore attended to." I admit the truth of the first part of this argument, as a desire of the acquisition of a knowledge of God is an indication of an improved mind; consequently whenever we see a person possessed of that desire, we should attribute it to some degree of purification; but I must affirm with the Véd, that purity of mind is the consequence of divine worship, and not of any superstitious practices.

The Vrihadaranyaca says, "Adore God alone." Again, "Nothing excepting the Supreme Being should "be adored by wise men."—"God alone rules the "mind, and relieves it from impurity."

The last of the principal arguments which are alleged in favour of idolatry is, that it is established by custom. "Let the authors of the Véds, Poorans, and

* Vide 10th chapter of the Gétá.

† Vide 23d text of the chap. 11th of the Débí-máhátmya.

‡ Vide Rudra máhátmya in the Dándharma.

"Tantras," it is said, "assert what they may in favour "of devotion to the Supreme Being, but idol worship "has been practised for so many centuries that custom "renders it proper to continue that worship." It is however evident to every one possessed of common sense, that custom or fashion is quite different from divine faith; the latter proceeding from spiritual authorities and correct reasoning, and the former being merely the fruit of vulgar caprice.

What can justify a man, who believes in the inspiration of his religious books, in neglecting the direct authorities of the same works, and subjecting himself entirely to custom and fashion, which are liable to perpetual changes and depend upon popular whim? But it cannot be passed unnoticed that those who practise idolatry and defend it under the shield of custom, have been violating their customs almost every twenty years, for the sake of a little convenience, or to promote their worldly advantage: a few instances which are most commonly and publicly practised, I beg leave to state here.

1st. The whole community in Bengal, with very few exceptions, have, since the middle of last century, forsaken their ancient modes of the performance of ceremonial rites of religion, and followed the precepts of the late Raghunandan, and consequently differ in the most essential points of ceremonies from the natives of Behar, Tirhoot, and Benares. 2d. The system of their subdivisions in each cast, with the modes of marriage and intermarriage, is also a modern introduction altogether contrary to their law and ancient customs. 3d. The profession of instructing European gentlemen in the Véds, Simrit and Purans, is a violation of their long established custom; and, 4th. The supplying their European guests with wine and victuals in presence of their gods and goddesses is also a direct breach of custom and law. I may conclude this subject with an appeal to the good sense of my countrymen, by asking them, "whose advice appears the most disinterested "and most rational—that of those who, concealing "your scriptures from you, continually teach you thus," 'Believe whatever we may say—don't examine or even 'touch your scriptures, neglect entirely your reasoning 'faculties—do not only consider us, whatever may be 'our principles, as gods on earth, but humbly adore 'and propitiate us by sacrificing to us the greater part '(if not the whole) of your property:' "or that of the "man who lays your scriptures and their comments as "well as their translations before you, and solicits you "to examine their purport, without neglecting the "proper and moderate use of reason; and to attend "strictly to their directions, by the rational perform- "ance of your duty to your sole Creator, and to your "fellow creatures, and also to pay true respect to those "who think and act righteously." I hope no one can be so prejudiced as to be unable to discern which advice is most calculated to lead him to the best road to both temporal and eternal happiness.

INTRODUCTION.

THE physical powers of man are limited, and when viewed comparatively, sink into insignificance; while in the same ratio, his moral faculties rise in our estimation, as embracing a wide sphere of action, and possessing a capability of almost boundless improvement. If the short duration of human life be contrasted with the great age of the universe, and the limited extent of bodily strength with the many objects to which there is a necessity of applying it, we must necessarily be disposed to entertain but a very humble opinion of our own nature; and nothing perhaps is so well calculated to restore our self-complacency as the contemplation of our more extensive moral powers, together with the highly beneficial objects which the appropriate exercise of them may produce.

On the other hand, sorrow and remorse can scarcely fail, sooner or later, to be the portion of him who is conscious of having neglected opportunities of rendering benefit to his fellow-creatures. From considerations like these it has been that I (although born a Brahmin, and instructed in my youth in all the principles of that sect), being thoroughly convinced of the lamentable errors of my countrymen, have been stimulated to employ every means in my power to improve their minds, and lead them to the knowledge of a purer system of morality. Living constantly amongst Hindoos of different sects and professions, I have had ample opportunity of observing the superstitious puerilities into which they have been thrown by their self-interested guides, who, in defiance of the law as well as of common sense, have succeeded but too well in conducting them to the temple of idolatry; and while they hid from their view the true substance of morality, have infused into their simple hearts a weak attachment for its mere shadow.

For the chief part of the theory and practice of Hindooism, I am sorry to say, is made to consist in the adoption of a peculiar mode of diet; the least aberration from which (even though the conduct of the offender may in other respects be pure and blameless) is not only visited with the severest censure, but actually punished by exclusion from the society of his family and friends. In a word, he is doomed to undergo what is commonly called loss of cast.

On the contrary, the rigid observance of this grand article of Hindoo faith is considered in so high a light as to compensate for every moral defect. Even the most atrocious crimes weigh little or nothing in the balance against the supposed guilt of its violation.

Murder, theft, or perjury, though brought home to the party by a judicial sentence, so far from inducing loss of cast, is visited in their society with no peculiar mark of infamy or disgrace.

A trifling present to the Brahmin, commonly called *Práyaschit*, with the performance of a few idle ceremonies, are held as a sufficient atonement for all those crimes; and the delinquent is at once freed from all temporal inconvenience, as well as all dread of future retribution.

My reflections upon these solemn truths have been most painful for many years. I have never ceased to contemplate with the strongest feelings of regret, the obstinate adherence of my countrymen to their fatal system of idolatry, inducing, for the sake of propitiating their supposed Deities, the violation of every humane and social feeling. And this in various instances; but more especially in the dreadful acts of self-destruction and the immolation of the nearest relations, under the delusion of conforming to sacred religious rites. I have never ceased, I repeat, to contemplate these practices with the strongest feelings of regret, and to view in them the moral debasement of a race who, I cannot help thinking, are capable of better things; whose susceptibility, patience, and mildness of character, render them worthy of a better destiny. Under these impressions, therefore, I have been impelled to lay before them genuine translations of parts of their scripture, which inculcates not only the enlightened worship of one God, but the purest principles of morality, accompanied with such notices as I deemed requisite to oppose the arguments employed by the Brahmins in defence of their beloved system. Most earnestly do I pray that the whole may, sooner or later, prove efficient in producing on the minds of Hindoos in general, a conviction of the rationality of believing in and adoring the Supreme Being only; together with a complete perception and practice of that grand and comprehensive moral principle—*Do unto others as ye would be done by.*

UPANISHAD

OF

THE VÉDA.

1st. ALL the material extension in this world, whatsoever it may be, should be considered as clothed with the existence of the Supreme regulating spirit: by thus abstracting thy mind *from worldly thoughts*, preserve thyself *from self-sufficiency*, and entertain not a covetous regard for property belonging to any individual.

2d. Let man desire to live a whole century, practising, in this world, during that time, religious rites; because for such A SELFISH MIND AS THINE, besides the observance of these rites, there is no other mode the practice of which would not subject thee to evils.

3d. THOSE THAT NEGLECT THE CONTEMPLATION OF THE SUPREME SPIRIT, *either by devoting themselves solely to the performance of the ceremonies of religion, or by living destitute of religious ideas, shall, after death*, ASSUME THE STATE OF DEMONS, *such as that of the celestial gods, and of other created beings*, WHICH ARE SURROUNDED WITH THE DARKNESS OF IGNORANCE.

4th. The Supreme Spirit is one and unchangeable: he proceeds more rapidly than the comprehending power of the mind: Him no external sense can apprehend, for a knowledge of him outruns even the internal sense: He, though free from motion, seems to advance, leaving behind human intellect, which strives to attain a knowledge respecting him: He being the eternal ruler, the atmosphere regulates under him the whole system of the world.

5th. He, the Supreme Being, seems to move every where, although he in reality has no motion; he seems to be distant *from those who have no wish to attain a knowledge respecting him*, and he seems to be near *to those who feel a wish to know him:* but, in fact, He pervades the internal and external parts of this whole universe.

6th. He, who perceives the whole universe in the Supreme Being (*that is, he who perceives that the material existence is merely dependent upon the existence of the Supreme Spirit*); and who also perceives the Supreme Being in the whole universe (*that is, he who perceives that the Supreme Spirit extends over all material extension*); does not feel contempt *towards any creature whatsoever*.

7th. When a person possessed of true knowledge conceives that God extends over the whole universe (*that is, that God furnishes every particle of the universe with the light of his existence*), how can he, as an observer of the real unity of the pervading Supreme existence, be affected with infatuation or grievance?

8th. He overspreads all creatures: is merely spirit, without the form either of any minute body, or of an extended one, which is liable to impression or organization: He is pure, perfect, omniscient, the ruler of the intellect, omnipresent, and the self-existent: He has from eternity been assigning to all creatures their respective purposes.

9th. Those observers of religious rites that perform only the worship of the sacred fire, and oblations to sages, to ancestors, to men, and to other creatures, without regarding the worship of celestial gods, shall enter into the dark regions: and those practisers of religious ceremonies who habitually worship the celestial gods only, disregarding the worship of the sacred fire, and oblations to sages, to ancestors, to men, and to other creatures, shall enter into a region still darker than the former.

10th. It is said that adoration of the celestial gods produces one consequence; and that the performance of the worship of sacred fire, and oblations to sages, to ancestors, to men, and to other creatures, produce another: thus have we heard from learned men who have distinctly explained the subject to us.

11th. Of those observers of ceremonies whosoever, knowing that adoration of celestial gods, as well as the worship of the sacred fire, and oblation to sages, to ancestors, to men, and to other creatures, should be observed alike by the same individual, performs them both, will, by means of the latter, surmount the obstacles presented by natural temptations, and will attain the state of the celestial gods through the practice of the former.

12th. Those observers of religious rites who worship Prakriti* alone, shall enter into the dark region: and those practisers of religious ceremonies that are devoted to worship solely the prior operating sensitive particle,

* Prakriti (or nature) who, though insensible, influenced by the Supreme Spirit, operates throughout the universe.

allegorically called Brahmá, shall enter into a region much more dark than the former.

13th. It is said that one consequence may be attained by the worship of Brahmá, and another by the adoration of Prakriti. Thus have we heard from learned men, who have distinctly explained the subject to us.

14th. Of those observers of ceremonies, whatever person, knowing that the adoration of Prakriti and that of Brahmá should be together observed by the same individual, performs them both, will by means of the latter overcome indigence, and will attain the state of Prakriti, through the practice of the former.

15. "Thou hast, O sun," (*says to the sun a person agitated on the approach of death, who during his life attended to the performance of religious rites, neglecting the attainment of a knowledge of God,*) "thou hast, O "Sun, concealed by thy illuminating body the way to "the true Being, who rules in thee. Take off that "veil for the guidance of me thy true devotee."

16th. "O thou" (continues he), "who nourishest "the *world*, movest singly, and who dost regulate the "*whole mundane* system—O sun, son of Cushyup, dis- "perse thy rays for my passage, and withdraw thy "violent light, so that I may by thy grace behold thy "most prosperous aspect."—"*Why should I*" (*says he, again retracting himself on reflecting upon the true di- "vine nature*), *why should I entreat the sun, as* I AM WHAT "HE IS," *that is,* "*the Being who rules in the sun rules "also in me.*"

17th. "Let my breath," *resumes he,* "be absorbed "*after death* into the wide atmosphere; and let this "my body be burnt to ashes. O my intellect, think

" *now on what may be beneficial to me.* O fire, remem-
" ber what religious rites I have hitherto performed."

18th. " O illuminating fire," *continues he*, " observ-
" ing all our religious practices, carry us by the right
" path to the enjoyment of the consequence of our
" deeds, and put an end to our sins; we being now
" unable to perform thy various rites, offer to thee our
" last salutation."*

* This example from the Véds, of the unhappy agitation and wavering of an idolater on the approach of death, ought to make men reflect seriously on the miserable consequence of fixing their mind on any other object of adoration but the one Supreme Being.

A
TRANSLATION INTO ENGLISH
OF A
SUNGSKRIT TRACT,
INCULCATING
THE DIVINE WORSHIP;
ESTEEMED
BY THOSE WHO BELIEVE IN THE REVELATION OF THE VEDS AS MOST APPROPRIATE TO THE NATURE OF
THE SUPREME BEING.

CALCUTTA:
1827.

PRESCRIPT

FOR

OFFERING SUPREME WORSHIP

BY MEANS OF

THE GAYUTREE,

THE MOST SACRED TEXT OF THE VEDS.

Thus says the illustrious Munoo: "The three great "immutable words (Bhooh, Bhoovuh, Swuh, or earth, "space, heaven), preceded by the letter Om;* and

* Om, when considered as one letter uttered by the help of one articulation, is the symbol of the Supreme Spirit. It is derived from the radical अव to preserve, with the affix मन्. "One "letter (Om) is the emblem of the Most High."—*Munoo*, II. 83. "This one letter, Om, is the emblem of the Supreme Being."—*Bhuguvudgeeta*. It is true that this emblem conveys two sounds, that of *o* and of *m*, nevertheless it is held to be one letter in the above sense; and we meet with instances even in the ancient and modern languages of Europe that can justify such privileges; such as Ξ and Ψ, reckoned single letters in Greek, and Q, W, X, in English and others. But when considered as a triliteral word consisting of अ, उ, म्, Om implies the three Veds, the three states of human nature, the three divisions of the universe, and the three deities, Bruhma, Vishnu and Shivu, agents in the creation, preservation, and destruction of this world; or, properly speaking, the three principal attributes of the Supreme Being personified as Bruhma, Vishnu, and Shivu. In this sense it implies, in fact, the universe controlled by the Supreme Spirit.

In

"also the Gayutree, consisting of three measured "lines, must be considered as the entrance to divine "bliss."*

"Whoever shall repeat them day by day, for three "years, without negligence, shall approach the most "High God, become *free* as air, and *acquire after death* "an ethereal essence."

"From the three Veds the most exalted Bruhma "successively milked out the three lines of this sacred "text, beginning with *the word* Tut and entitled Savi-"tree or Gayutree."

Yogee Yajnuvulkyu also declares, "By means of "Om; Bhooh, Bhoovuh, and Swuh; and the Gayu-"tree, collectively or each of the three singly, the most "High God, the source of intellect, should be wor-"shipped."

"So Bruhma himself formerly defined Bhooh,

In all the Hindoo treatises of philosophy (the Poorans or didactic parables excepted), the methodical collection or expansion of matter is understood by the term creation, the gradual or sudden perversion of order is intended by destruction, and the power which wards off the latter from the former is meant by preservation.

The reason the authors offer for this interpretation is, that they, in common with others, are able to acquire a notion of a Superintending Power, though unfelt and invisible, solely through their observation of material phenomena; aud that should they reject this medium of conviction, and force upon themselves a belief of the production of matter from nothing, and of its liability to entire annihilation, then nothing would remain in the ordinary course of reasoning to justify their maintaining any longer a notion of that unknown Supreme Superintending Power.

* The last clause admits of another interpretation, *viz.* "must "be considered as the mouth, *or principal part* of the Veds."

"Bhoovuh, Swuh, (Earth, Space, Heaven) as the "body of the Supreme Intelligence; hence these *three* "*words* are called the Defined."

[Those that maintain the doctrine of the universe being the body of the Supreme Spirit, found their opinion upon the following considerations:

1st. That there are innumerable millions of bodies, properly speaking worlds, in the infinity of space.

2dly. That they move, mutually preserving their regular intervals between each other, and that they maintain each other by producing effects primary or secondary, as the members of the body support each other.

3dly. That those bodies, when viewed collectively, are considered one; in the same way as the members of an animal body or of a machine, taken together, constitute one whole.

4thly. Any material body whose members move methodically, and afford support to each other in a manner sufficient for their preservation, must be actuated either by an internal guiding power named the soul, or by an external one as impulse.

5thly. It is maintained that body is as infinite as space, because body is found to exist in space as far as our perceptions, with the naked eye or by the aid of instruments, enable us to penetrate.

6thly. If body be infinite as space, the power that guides its members must be internal, and therefore styled the SOUL, and not external, since there can be no existence, even in thought, without the idea of location.

Hence this sect suppose that the Supreme all-pervading power is the soul of the universe, both existing from eternity to eternity; and that the former has somewhat the same influence over the universe as the individual soul has over the individual body.

They argue further, that in proportion as the internally impelled body is excellent in its construction, the directing soul must be considered excellent. Therefore, inasmuch as the universe is infinite in extent, and is arranged with infinite skill, the soul by which it is animated must be infinite in every perfection.]

He (Yajnuvulkyu) again expounds the meaning of the Gayutree in three passages:

"We, say the adorers of the Most High, meditate "on the Supreme and omnipresent internal spirit of "this splendid Sun. We meditate on the same "Supreme spirit, earnestly sought for by such as dread "further mortal birth; who, residing in every body as "the all-pervading soul and controller of the mind, "constantly directs our intellect and intellectual ope-"rations towards *the acquisition of* virtue, wealth, phy-"sical enjoyment, and final beatitude."

So, at the end of the Gayutree, the utterance of the letter Om is commanded by the sacred passage cited by Goonu-Vishnoo: "A Brahmun shall in "every instance pronounce Om, at the beginning and "at the end; for unless the letter Om precede, *the* "*desirable consequence* will fail; and unless it follow, it "will not be long retained."

That the letter Om, which is pronounced at the beginning and at the end *of the Gayutree*, expressly signifies the Most High, is testified by the Ved: *viz.* "Thus through the help of Om, you contemplate the "Supreme Spirit." (*Moonduk Oopunishud.*)

Munoo also calls to mind the purport of the same passage: " All rites ordained in the Ved, such as ob-" lation to fire and solemn offerings, pass away; but " the letter Om is considered that which passes not " away; since it is *a symbol of* the most High the Lord " of created beings."

" By the sole repetition *of Om and the Gayutree*, " a Brahmun may indubitably attain beatitude. Let " him perform or not perform any other religious rites, " he being a friend *to all creatures* is styled a knower of " God."

So Yogee Yajnuvulkyu says: " God is declared to " be the object signified, and Om to be the term sig-" nifying: By means of a knowledge even of the letter " Om, the symbol, God becomes propitious."

In the Bhuguvudgeeta: " Om* (the cause), Tut† " (that), Sut‡ (existing), these are considered three " kinds of description of the supreme Being."

* " Om" implies the Being on whom all objects, either visible or invisible, depend in their formation, continuance, and change.

† " Tut" implies the being that can be described only by the demonstrative pronoun " that," and not by any particular defination.

‡ " Sut" implies what " truly exists" in one condition independent of others. These three terms collectively imply, that the object contemplated through " Om" can be described only as " that" which " is existing."

The first term " Om" bears a striking similarity, both in sound and application, to the participle " ων" of the verb "ειμι" *to be*, in Greek; and it is therefore not very improbable that one might have had its origin from the other. As to the similarity in sound, it is too obvious to require illustration; and a reference to the Septuagint will shew that ων like " Om" is applied to Jehova the ever existing God. Exodus, iii. 14. " Εγω ειμι ὁ Ων." " ὁ Ων απεσταλκε με προς ὑμας."

In the concluding part of the commentary on the Gayutree by the ancient Bhuttu Goonu-Vishnoo, the meaning of the passage is briefly given by the same author.

" He, the spirit who is thus described, guides us. " He, as the soul of the three mansions (*viz.* earth, " space, and heaven), of water, light, moisture, and " the individual soul, of all moving and fixed objects; " and of Bruhma, Vishnoo, Shivu, the Sun, and other " gods of various descriptions, the Most High God, " illuminating, like a brilliant lamp, the seven man- " sions, having carried my individual soul, as spirit, to " the seventh heaven, the mansion of the worshippers " of God called the True mansion, the residence of " Bruhma, absorbs it (my soul), through his divine " spirit, into his own divine essence. The worshipper, " thus contemplating, shall repeat the Gayutree."

Thus it is said by Rughoonundun Bhuttacharyu, a modern expounder of law in the country of Gourr, when interpreting the passage beginning with " Prunuvu Vyahritibhyam:"—" By means of pronouncing " Om and Bhooh, Bhoovuh, Swuh, and the Gayutree, " all signifying the Most High, and reflecting on their " meaning, the worship of God shall be performed, and " his grace enjoyed."

And also in the Muha Nirvan Tuntru: " In like " manner, among all texts the Gayutree is declared to " be the most excellent: the worshipper shall repeat it " when inwardly pure, reflecting on the meaning of it. " If the Gayutree be repeated with Om and the Vyah- " riti (*viz.* Bhooh, Bhoovuh, Swuh), it excels all other " theistical knowledge, in producing immediate bliss.

"Whosoever repeats it in the morning or evening or "during the night, while meditating on the Supreme "Being, being freed from all past sins, shall not be "inclined to act unrighteously. The worshipper shall "first pronounce Om, then the three Vyahritis, and "afterwards the Gayutree of three lines, and shall "finish it with the term Om. We meditate on him "from whom proceed the continuance, perishing, and "production *of all things;* who spreads over the three "mansions; that eternal Spirit, who inwardly rules the "sun and all living creatures; most desirable and all-"pervading; and who, residing in intellect, directs the "operations of the intellectual power of all of us mate-"rial beings. The worshipper, by repeating every day "these three texts expressing the above meaning, "attains all desirable objects, without any other reli-"gious observance or austerity. 'One only without a "'second' is the doctrine maintained by all the Oopuni-"shuds: that imperishable and incomprehensible Being "is understood by these three texts. Whoever repeats "them once, or ten, or a hundred times, either alone or "with many others, attains bliss in a proportionate "degree. After he has completed the repetition, he "shall again meditate on Him who is one only without "a second, and all-pervading: thereby all religious "observances, though not performed, shall have been "virtually performed. Any one, whether a house-"holder or not, whether a Brahmun or not, all have "equal right to the use of these texts as found in the "Tuntru."

Here Om, in the first instance, signifies that Supreme Being who is the sole cause of the continuance, perishing, and production of all worlds. "He from whom "these creatures are produced, by whom those that are "produced exist, and to whom after death they return, "is the Supreme Being, whom thou dost seek to know." —The text of the Ved quoted by the revered Shunkur Acharyu in the Commentary on the first text of the Vedant Durshun.

The doubt whether or not that cause signified by "Om" exists separately from these effects, having arisen, the second text, Bhoor Bhoovuh Swuh, is next read, explaining that God, the sole cause, eternally exists pervading the universe, "Glorious, invisible, "perfect, unbegotten, pervading all, internally and "externally is He *the Supreme spirit*."—*Moonduk Oopunishud.*

It being still doubted whether or not living creatures large and small in the world act independently of that sole cause, the Gayutree, as the third in order, is read. "Tut Suvitoor vurenyum, Bhurgo devusyu dheemuhi, "dhiyo yo nuh pruchoduyat." We meditate on that indescribable spirit inwardly ruling the splendid Sun, the express object *of worship*. He does not only inwardly rule the sun, but he, the spirit, residing in and inwardly ruling all us material beings, directs mental operations towards their objects. "He who inwardly "rules the sun is the same immortal spirit who inwardly "rules thee." (*Chhandoggu Oopunishud.*)—"God resides "in the heart of all creatures."—*Bhuguvudgeeta.*

The object signified by the three texts being one, their repetition collectively is enjoined. The following is their meaning in brief.

"We meditate on the cause of all, pervading all, and

" internally ruling all material objects, from the sun " down to us and others."

[The following is a literal translation of the Gayutree according to the English idiom: " We meditate on " that Supreme Spirit of the splendid sun who directs " our understandings."

The passage, however, may be rendered somewhat differently by transferring the demonstrative "that" from the words "Supreme Spirit" to the words " splendid sun." But this does not appear fully to correspond with the above interpretation of Yajnuvulkyu.]

While translating this essay on the Gayutree, I deemed it proper to refer to the meaning of the text as given by Sir William Jones; whose talents, acquisitions, virtuous life, and impartial research, have rendered his memory an object of love and veneration to all. I feel so much delighted by the excellence of the translation, or rather the paraphrase given by that illustrious character, that with a view to connect his name and his explanation of the passage with this humble treatise, I take the liberty of quoting it here.

The interpretation in question is as follows:

" THE GAYATRI, OR HOLIEST VERSE OF THE VEDAS."

" Let us adore the supremacy of *that* divine sun,* " the godhead† who illuminates all, who recreates all,

* Opposed to the visible luminary.

† *Bhargas*, a word consisting of three consonants, derived from *bhá*, to shine; *ram*, to delight; *gam*, to move.

"from whom all proceed, to whom all must return,
"whom we invoke to direct our understandings aright
"in our progress toward his holy seat.

* * * * * *

"What the sun and light are to this visible world, "that are the *Supreme good* and *truth* to the intel-"lectual and invisible universe; and, as our corporeal "eyes have a distinct perception of objects enlightened "by the sun, thus our souls acquire certain knowledge, "by meditating on the light of truth, which emanates "from the Being of beings: *that* is the light by which "alone our minds can be directed in the path to bea-"titude."

A DEFENCE

OF

HINDOO THEISM,

IN REPLY TO THE

ATTACK OF AN ADVOCATE FOR IDOLATRY

AT MADRAS.

CALCUTTA:
1827.

PREFACE

THE following sheets contain some remarks in reply to a publication which appeared in the "Madras Courier" of November last, under the signature of Sankara Sastri, in answer to my abridgment of the Vedant and my Preface to the translation of the Ishopanishad, as well as to my Introduction to the Cenopanishad. The length to which the arguments of the controvertist extended having precluded their appearance in the Calcutta prints, I have taken the liberty of reprinting them along with my own observations on them, in order that the discussion may be brought fully before the public, to whose decision the merits of the question must now be left.

TO THE

EDITOR OF THE MADRAS COURIER.

SIR,

On reading your paper, dated 19th November 1816, I found a publication in it taken from a Calcutta paper, respecting the theological doctrines of RAM MOHUN ROY, on which I shall proceed to make a few observations.

In the first part of this publication it is stated: "this "eminently learned and indefatigable reformer is pro- "ceeding, with unremitting exertions, in the laudable "work of enlightening his countrymen, and reclaiming "them from their debasing system of idolatry. Having, "for the instruction of the Hindu population of these "provinces, translated into Bengalese the principal "chapters of the Veds, he has now done a few of them "into English, for the gratification of such European "gentlemen as interest themselves in the improvement "of their fellow-creatures."

In a former paper, also, it was stated that the learned person here mentioned, had "*discovered*" that the doctrine of the Unity of the Godhead was taught in the Puránas and Tantras as well as the Vedas.

The worship of the All-pervading and Supreme Being is the original doctrine founded on the Vedas,

Purnas, &c., and is known in general in this, as well as in the other parts of the Peninsula:—this faith is known by the name of *Adwaitam*, which being derived from *dwita* duality, by affixing the privative *a* is the opposite of *dwiatam*, the term usually applied to the belief that admits of more than one first cause: it is impossible to say when it was first revealed, yet, among various conjectures, the probability is, that the revelation of this faith is to be ascribed to Brahmá, the creating power alone, and that it is as ancient, therefore, as the existence of the world.

People of limited understanding, not being able to comprehend the system of worshipping the Invisible Being, have adopted doctrines, and by that means confounded weak minds in remote times; but due punishment was inflicted on those heretics, and religion was very well established throughout India by the Reverend SENKARACHARYAM and his disciples, who, however, did not pretend to *reform or discover* them, or assume the title of a *reformer* or *discoverer*.

There are an immense number of books, namely, Vedas, Sastras, Puranas Agams, Tantras-Sutras, and Itihas, besides numerous commentaries compiled by many famous theologians, both of ancient and modern times, respecting the doctrine of the worship of the Invisible Being. They are not only written in Sanscrit, but rendered into Pracruta, Tenugu, Tamil, Guzerat, Hindoostani, Maratta, Canari, &c. languages, and immemorially studied by a great part of the Hindu nation attached to the Adwaitam faith, and so our ancestors left no room to any person to make "*discoveries*" on the subject, or "to *proceed with unremitting exertion in* "*the laudable work of enlightening his countrymen, and* "*reclaiming them from their debasing system of idolatry.*"

From my stating these doctrines to have been anciently translated, I beg it may not be construed that those translations are universally admitted. On the contrary, they are rejected by some and admitted by others, for reason recited as follows :—

First.—If the reader of them doubts the truth of the principles explained in the translation, the divine knowledge he acquired by them becomes a doubtful faith, and that doubt cannot be removed unless he compare them with the original work ; in that case the knowledge he lastly acquired becomes superior, and his study in the first instance becomes useless, and the cause of repeating the same work.

Second.—Reading the Scriptures in the vulgar languages is prohibited by the Puranas.

Third.—These translations are omitted by others as useful and interesting in general, and particularly to those who have not sufficient knowledge in Sanscrit.

Not wishing to trouble my readers with the observations necessary to reconcile these three controversial points, I think it proper to leave it to them to judge which of them is admissible.

The Sútra Bhashyam, or the Commentary on the Theological Sutrams of Veda Vyasa, and those on the Uponishets, &c. are in this part of India constantly read and taught by the Brahmins all over the country. Lectures and themes are delivered in the various audiences frequently and purposely held by the Rajahs, Pundits, and other respectable men in the country. The ascribing of the "*discovery*" of a religious tenet so well known and celebrated, to a learned native, cannot therefore be here admitted by a Hindu, and he will not be more astonished at it than he would at hearing that a man had one head and two eyes.

Previously to my proceeding to make any observations respecting idolatrous worship, I think it proper to state how the Supreme Being is defined.

The Vedas, Purans, &c. say that this Being is infinite, eternal, self-intelligent, indivisible, inconsumable, pervading, universal, inconceivable, invisible, unalterable, and almighty. It is not subject either to the mind or senses. The translation of the following Sanscrit slokams will serve to form an idea of its nature.

" He is eternal, he is the splendour of splendour.

" He is supreme and glorious.

" The sun shines not with respect to him, nor the " moon nor fire."

" Thou hearest without ears,
" Thou smellest without a nose,
" Thou walkest without legs,
" Thou seest without eyes,
" Thou tastest without a tongue.

" Thou hast no gotram, nor birth, nor name, nor " shape, nor state, nor place.

" Though thou art thus, yet thou art the Lord of " the earth and the heaven.

" In the same manner as the illusive appearance of " water, produced by the reflection of the rays in the " mirage :

" So the universe shines in thee, the real and intel- " ligent spirit."

" Thou canst not be known either by the organs or
" by the mind, as thou art self-resplendent and distinct
" from elemental being.

" If ignorance be annihilated by knowledge, as dark-
" ness by the dawn, thy light will shine like the sun."

" The whole had its birth in thee,
" The whole rests in thee.
" The whole obtains its destruction in thee, like
" bubbles in water."

The difficulty of attaining the knowledge of this invisible and Almighty Spirit, is evident from the preceding verses, and all the Scriptures and other authorities affirm that the soul, propelled by Maya towards external objects, and obscured by the ignorance of individuality, cannot obtain *mocaham* (salvation) unless it is freed from every impression either of vice and virtue, the illusions of Maya; and until that time, it will continue to undergo various transmigrations, and partake of misery and happiness, the result of its vices and virtues, in the terrestrial, celestial, and infernal worlds.

The eating food, slumbering, fear, love, and other animal functions and propensities, are common and natural both to the human and brute creation; they both seek for food and are subject to slumber. Out of the fear of death, &c. they either attack or fly when opposed by an enemy; but though the intellectual powers of both races are the same in general, and entirely directed towards external objects, yet one human race is endowed with the powers of reason and determination. These, if applied, serve to reason—who is himself? from whence he is come? what is the connexion between him and the Supreme Being? how the spirit in him is illusively inspired, and illusively beheld, and illusively divided from the pervading spirit.

The mental powers of every corporeal being are, from the time of its birth, attracted by external objects, and they cannot be inverted towards the individual spirit, or the object meant by the word "I," without great labour, practice, mental exercise, purification, and the divine assistance, or favouring grace, of the Deity, without which a complete knowledge of his *atmá* or spirit cannot be obtained.

It is said in the Scripture, that the person void of this knowledge does not only remain self-ignorant, but it is decreed by the authorities that he is a self-deceiver, and his ignorance finally proves fatal to himself.

In order to save the human race from the utter destruction occasioned by self-ignorance, Brahámá delivered the divine precepts in the Védas, both for the use of men of enlightened and limited understanding. These precepts are divided into two parts, namely, Carmocándam, òr works, and Gnanacandam, or knowledge, or faith, as European writers express it; these words I understand to mean essentially the same thing, for what is faith without adequacy of knowledge?

The first prescribes the mode of performing Yagam or Sacrifice, bestowing Danam or Alms, treats of penance, fasting, and of worshipping the Incarnations, in which the Supreme Deity has appeared on the earth for divine purposes. The ceremonies performed according to these modes, forsaking their fruits, are affirmed by the Védas to be mental exercises and mental purifications, necessary to obtain the knowledge of the divine nature.

The latter part treats on Theology and Metaphysics, on the nature of spirit, of mental abstraction, the subjugation of the passions, &c., the meaning of which the student must attain by reasoning, and must impress it well on the understanding by reflection; he must behold the Supreme Spirit alike in all things; he must constantly contemplate the union of his own *atmá*, or soul, with the Universal Supreme Spirit, which he must consider unconnected though in all connections, and inactive in all things in action, and must comprehend the whole universe in him alone. The Gnani, or the man that has attained divine knowledge in this manner, should be unaffected in all his actions; the same in praise and insult, in friendship and in enmity, in honour and dishonour, in pleasure and pain, in cold and heat; all his passions should be subdued, and his mind constantly fixed and united with the universal Spirit.

I must here introduce another extract from the publication to which I have referred. "We understand that "on all the great Hindoo festivals the *Friendly Society*, "established by him, holds meetings, not only with the "view that its members may keep aloof from the idolatrous ceremonies of their countrymen, but also to "renew and strengthen their own faith in the purer "doctrines which they affirm to be established in the "Veds. At these meetings they have music and dancing, as well as their more superstitious brethren; "but the songs are all expressive of the peculiar tenets "of the Monotheists."

It is evident from what is said above of the precepts in the Védam, that divine knowledge cannot be obtained without purifying the soul, and such purification cannot take place without performing Yagams, bestowing Danams, by penance, worship, reading theology, and comprehending and reasoning on its meaning; but the *holding of meetings, playing music, singing songs and dancing*, which are ranked among carnal pleasures, are not ordained by scripture as mental purification.

It may be asked why purification cannot be attained by these songs, music, &c. since they are all intended to be expressive of the tenets of Monotheism? I answer, that the completion of every undertaking in the world must take place by its respective means: for example, the thirst must be quenched by water, milk, and such like, but not with sand. These, the aforesaid means for quenching thirst, are known by human experience and usage: but the means to purify the unknown and invisible powers of the intellect cannot be ascertained by human understanding, but by the precepts revealed by divine wisdom. Therefore, the setting aside the proper means, such as Yagam, penance, worship, &c., and substituting dancing, music, and songs, appear in no way preferable by any doctrine.

What has hitherto been said, applies only to the observations of the writer in the Calcutta Paper, for which RAM MOHUN ROY cannot be answerable; I must, however, make a few remarks on the "Introduction," as it is stated to be, to his "translation of "one of the chapters of the Sama Véda." The author states that it is "a general characteristic of each Ved, "that the primary chapters of each branch treat of

" astronomy, medicine, arms, and other arts and " sciences." All the Brahmans in this part of the Peninsula are studying the same Védams as are read in the other part of the country, but I do not recollect to have read or heard of one treating on astronomy, medicine, or arms: the first is indeed an Angan of the Vedam, but the two latter are taught in separate Sastras.

The author continues—" they also exhibit allegori- " cal representation of the attributes of the Supreme " Being by means of earthly objects," &c.; he then proceeds to state that the worship of these, as explained in the Véds, was " inculcated only for the sake of those " whose limited understandings rendered them inca- " pable of comprehending and adoring the invisible " Supreme Being." He does not appear satisfied, however, with this explanation; he seems to think it may not be thought sufficient to reconcile the doctrines of the two portions of the Véds, and he admits, that, if it is not, " the whole work must not only be stripped " of its authority, but looked upon as altogether un- " intelligible." To say the least of this passage, RAM MOHUN ROY appears quite as willing to abandon as to defend the Scripture of his religion: but let us examine if it be necessary to abandon them so readily.

The attributes in the preceding extract are affirmed by the Védas to be the creating, protecting, destroying, and the like powers or incarnations of the Supreme Being. Their worship, under various representations, by means of consecrated objects, is prescribed by the scripture to the human race by way of mental exercise, who, owing to the waving nature of their minds, cannot without assistance, fix their thoughts on the incomprehensible and Almighty Being. Though the representations of the attributes are allegorical, yet the pervading nature of the Supreme Being in the attributes, in their representations, and in the objects dedicated to them, is not allegorical, and I regard the same as an ether diffused throughout ten thousand objects. If this reasoning be admitted, why cannot the prayer offered to the All-pervading Spirit in the dedicated object be considered as prayer to the universal and ALMIGHTY GOD?—If one part of the ocean be adored, the whole ocean is adored.

If a person be desirous to visit an earthly prince, he ought to be introduced, in the first instance, by his ministers, but not of himself to rush in upon him at once, regardless of offending him; should a man wish to ascend a flight of stairs, he ought to proceed step by step, and not to leap up several at a time, so as to endanger the wounding of his legs. In like manner the grace of GOD ought to be obtained by degrees, through the worship of his attributes.

I have further to observe, by way of example, that although the milk pervades the whole body of a cow, yet it is to be drawn only from the teats; so though the Supreme Being pervades all, yet his mercy is obtained through the worship of his attributes, to which a special energy is ascribed by the Scripture. The worshippers are assured by the Védas that the particular energy inherent in the attributes will crown their wishes, provided their zeal and their faith be unaltered and steady.

The objections to worshipping the attributes are not

satisfactorily stated by the author, but it seems that it is his general idea that it is not a worship directly to the Supreme Being, and that it is not prescribed in the Scriptures of certain nations. As to the last objection it is clear, however, that the worship of the attributes is not merely not rejected, but prescribed by the Scriptures of our religion; here is the difference, and as the deliverers of the Scripture, of any religion, are not of a nature to be seen or spoken to for the purpose of proving their validity, the truth of either opinion can only be established by analogy, inference, and other modes of logic.

If the worship of the attributes be rejected, what means can be substituted to inculcate the truth and to enlighten the understanding of an indolent man, who on being told that the God is all-pervading and invisible, thinks him to be like the air, or the sky; or hearing that, by a figure of speech, he is called the splendour of splendour, believes that he is of a luminous nature? If these helps be denied him, will he not at last become ignorant of the true faith, or be induced to follow atheistical doctrines, rather than to trouble his head to attain the difficult knowledge of the divine nature?

I have lastly to observe that, according to the Christian doctrine of the Trinity, or the three persons in the Godhead, though one and united yet are personally, or occasionally, distinguished, and prayers offered to the Godhead are concluded by the words "through "Jesus Christ our Saviour." I believe, though I may be mistaken, that the Saviour should be considered a personification of the mercy and kindness of God (I mean actual, not allegorical personification; pure allegory I leave to RAM MOHUN ROY)—if this be so, is not mercy an attribute of GOD? Is not the prayer offered to him, through his attribute, of the same nature as the worship of the Hindus? Do not the votaries of the Christian religion, like the Hindus, acknowledge him to be essentially united to the Godhead, though occasionally separate, and do they not believe that they are certain of obtaining salvation in this faith?

For these reasons, why cannot the Hindu worship of the attributes, which are affirmed to be essentially united, but occasionally separate from the Godhead, be admitted, and why may not this be the means of obtaining *moscham* or salvation? It seems upon the whole that technical terms, modes of worship, and external rights, respectively observed, constitute an apparent difference between the religions of the earth, though in truth there be none.

I am, Sir,
Your most obedient humble servant,
B. SENKARA SASTRI,
Head English Master in the
College of Fort St. George.

Madras, 26th December 1816.

Before I attempt to reply to the observations that the learned gentleman, who signs himself Senkara Sastri, has offered in his letter of the 20th December last, addressed to the Editor of the Madras Courier, on the subject of an article published in the Calcutta Gazette, and on my translation of an abridgment of the Védánta and of the two chapters of the Védas; I beg to be allowed to express the disappointment I have felt, in receiving from a learned Brahman controversial remarks on Hindoo Theology, written in a foreign language; as it is the invariable practice of the natives of all provinces of Hindoostan to hold their discussions on such subjects in Sangscrit, which is the learned language common to all of them, and in which they may naturally be expected to convey their ideas with perfect correctness, and greater facility than in any foreign tongue: nor need it be alleged that, by adopting this established channel of controversy, the opportunity of appealing to public opinion on the subject must be lost; as a subsequent translation from the Sungscrit into English may sufficiently serve that purpose. The irregularity of this mode of proceeding, however, gives me room to suspect that the letter in question is the production of the pen of an English gentleman, whose liberality, *I suppose*, has induced him to attempt an apology, even for the absurd idolatry of his fellow-creatures. If this inference be correct, while I congratulate that gentleman on his progress in a knowledge of the sublime doctrines of the Védánta, I must, at the same time, take the liberty of entreating that he will, for the future, prefer consulting the original works written upon those doctrines, to relying on the second-hand information on the subject, that may be offered him by any person whatsoever.

The learned gentleman commences by objecting to the terms *discoverer* and *reformer*, in which the Editor of the Calcutta Gazette was pleased to make mention of me. He states, "that people of limited under-"standing, not being able to comprehend the system "of worshipping the invisible Being, have adopted "false doctrines, and by that means confounded weak "minds in remote times; but due punishment was "inflicted on those heretics, and religion was very well "established throughout India by the Reverend San-"karacharya and his disciples; who, however, did not "pretend to *reform* or *discover* them, or assume the "title of a *reformer* or *discoverer*." In none of my writings, nor in any verbal discussion, have I ever pretended to reform or to discover the doctrines of the unity of God, nor have I ever assumed the title of reformer or discoverer: so far from such an assumption, I have urged in every work that I have hitherto published, that the doctrines of the unity of God are real Hindooism, as that religion was practised by our ancestors, and as it is well known even at the present age to many learned Brahmins: I beg to repeat a few of the passages to which I allude.

In the introduction to the abridgment of the Védánta I have said: "In order, therefore, to vindicate my "own faith and that of *our forefathers*, I have been "endeavouring, for some time past, to convince my "countrymen of the *true meaning of our sacred* books; "and prove that my aberration deserves not the oppro-

"brium, which some unreflecting persons have been "so ready to throw upon me." In another place of the same introduction: "The present is an endeavour "to render an abridgment of the same (the Védánta) "into English; by which I expect to prove to my "European friends, that the superstitious practices "which deform the Hindoo religion, have nothing to "do with the pure spirit of its dictates." In the introduction of the Cenopanishad: "This work will, I trust, "by explaining to my countrymen *the real spirit of the "Hindoo scriptures, which is but the declaration of the "unity of God,* tend in a great degree to correct the "erroneous conceptions which have prevailed with "regard to the doctrines they inculcate;" and in the Preface of the Ishopanished: "*many learned Brahmins* "are perfectly aware of the absurdity of idol worship, "and *are well informed of the nature of the pure mode of "divine worship.*" A reconsideration of these passages will, I hope, convince the learned gentleman, that I never advanced any claim to the title either of a reformer, or of a discoverer of the doctrines of the unity of the Godhead. It is not at all impossible that from the perusal of the translations above alluded to, the Editor of the Calcutta Gazette, finding the system of idolatry into which Hindoos are now completely sunk, quite inconsistent with the real spirit of their scriptures, may have imagined that their contents had become entirely forgotten and unknown; and that I was the first to point out the absurdity of idol worship, and to inculcate the propriety of the pure divine worship, ordained by their Védas, their Smrits, and their Poorans. From this idea, and from finding in his intercourse with other Hindoos, that I was stigmatized by many, however unjustly, as an *innovator*, he may have been, not unnaturally, misled to apply to me the epithets of discoverer and reformer.

2dly. The learned gentleman states: "There are "an immense number of books, namely, *Védas*, Sastras, "Poorans, Agams, Tantras, Sutras, and Itihas, besides "numerous commentaries compiled by many famous "theologians, both of ancient and modern times, "respecting the doctrines of the worship of the invisible "Being. They are not only written in Sangscrit, "but rendered into the Pracreta, Tenuga, Tamol, "Gujrate, Hindoostani, Marhutta, and Canari lan-"guages, and immemorially studied by a great part of "the Hindu nation, attached to the adwaitum faith, "&c." This statement of the learned gentleman, as far as it is correct, corroborates indeed my assertion with respect to the doctrines of the worship of the invisible Supreme Spirit being unanimously inculcated by all the Hindoo Sastras, and naturally leads to severe reflections on the selfishness which must actuate those Braminical teachers who, notwithstanding the unanimous authority of the Sastras for the adoption of pure worship, yet, with the view of maintaining the title of God, which they arrogate to themselves, and of deriving pecuniary and other advantages from the numerous rites and festivals of idol worship, constantly advance and encourage idolatry to the utmost of their power. I must remark, however, that there is no translation of the Védas into any of the modern languages of Hindoostan with which I am acquainted, and it is for that reason that I have translated into Bengali the Védánta, the Cenopanishad of the Sama Veda, Ishopanishad of the Yojur Véda, &c., with the contents of which none but the learned among my countrymen were at all acquainted.

3dly. The learned gentleman states that the translations of the scripture into the vulgar language are rejected by some people; and he assigns as reasons for their so doing, that "if the reader of them doubts the truth of "the principles explained in the translation, the divine "knowledge he acquired by them becomes a doubtful "faith, and that doubt cannot be removed unless he "compare them with the original work: in that case, "the knowledge he lastly acquired becomes superior, "and his study, in the first instance, becomes useless, "and the cause of repeating the same work." When a translation of a work written in a foreign tongue is made by a person at all acquainted with that language into his native tongue, and the same translation is sanctioned and approved of by many natives of the same country, who are perfectly conversant with that foreign language, the translation, I presume, may be received with confidence, as a satisfactory interpretation of the original work, both by the vulgar and by men of literature.

It must not be supposed, however, that I am inclined to assert that there is not the least room to doubt the accuracy of such a translation; because the meaning of authors, even in the original works, is very frequently dubious, especially in a language like Sungscrit, every sentence of which, almost, admits of being explained in different senses. But should the possibility of errors in every translation be admitted as reason for withholding all confidence in their contents, such a rule would shake our belief, not only in the principles explained in the translation of the Védánt into the current language, but also in all information respecting foreign history and theology obtained by means of translations: in that case, we must either learn all the languages that are spoken by the different nations in the world, to acquire a knowledge of their histories and religions, or be content to know nothing of any country besides our own. The second reason which the learned gentleman assigns for their objection to the translation is, that "Reading the scripture in the "vulgar languages is prohibited by the Poorans." I have not yet met with any texts of any Poorans which prohibit the explanation of the scriptures in the vulgar tongue; on the contrary, the Poorans allow that practice very frequently. I repeat one of these declarations from the Shiva Dhurma, quoted by the great Bughnund. "He who can interpret, according to "the ratio of the understanding of his pupils, through "Sunscrit, or through the vulgar languages, or by "means of the current language of the country, is "entitled, spiritual father." Moreover, in every part of Hindoostan all professors of the Sungscrit language instructing beginners in the Véds, Poorans, and in other sastras, interpret them in the vulgar languages; especially spiritual fathers in exposition of those parts of the veds and Poorans, which allegorically introduce a plurality of gods and idol-worship; doctrines which tend so much to their own worldly advantage.

The learned gentleman states, that "The first of "the Véda prescribes the mode of performing *yagam* "or sacrifice, bestowing *daneem* or alms; treats of "penance, fasting, and of worshipping the incarna- "tions, in which the Supreme Deity has appeared on "the earth for divine purposes. The ceremonies per- "formed according to these modes, forsaking their "fruits, are affirmed by the Védás to be mental exercises "and mental purifications necessary to obtain the know- "ledge of the divine nature." I, in common with the Védas and the Védánt, and Munoo (the first and best of Hindoo *lawgivers*) as well as with the most celebrated Sancharacharya, deny these ceremonies being necessary to obtain the knowledge of the divine nature; as the Védánt positively declares, in text 36, sec. 4th, chap. 3d: "Man may acquire the true knowledge "of God, even without observing the rules and rites "prescribed by the Véd for each class; as it is found "in the Véd that many persons who neglected the "performance of the rites and ceremonies, owing to "their perpetual attention to the adoration of the "Supreme Being, acquired the true knowledge re- "specting the Supreme Spirit." The Véd says: "Many learned true believers never worshipped fire, "or any celestial gods through fire." And also the Védánt asserts, in the 1st text of 3d sec. of the 3d chap.: "The worship authorized by all the Véds is "one, as the directions for the worship of the only "Supreme Being are invariably found in the Véd, and "the epithets of the Supreme and Omnipresent Being, "&c. commonly imply God alone." Munoo, as I have elsewhere quoted, thus declares on the same point, chap. 12th, text 92d: "Thus must the chief "of the twice born, though he neglect the ceremonial "rites mentioned in the Sastrà, be diligent in attaining "a knowledge of God, in controling his organs of "sense, and in repeating the Véd." Again, chapter 4th, text 23d: "Some constantly sacrifice their "breath in their speech, *when they instruct others "of God aloud*, and their speech in their breath, *when "they meditate in silence*; perceiving in their speech "and breath thus employed the imperishable fruit of "a sacrificial offering." 24th: "Other Brahmans in-"cessantly perform those sacrifices only; seeing with "the eye of divine learning, that the scriptural know-"ledge is the root of every ceremonial observance." And also the same author declares in the chap. 2d, text 84: "All rites ordained in the Véda, oblations to "fire and solemn sacrifices, pass away; but that which "passes not away is declared to be the syllable Om, "thence called Acshora; since it is a symbol of God, "the Lord of created beings."

5thly. The learned gentleman states, that "the "difficulty of attaining a knowledge of the Invisible "and Almighty Spirit is evident from the preceding "verses." I agree with him in that point; that the attainment of perfect knowledge of the nature of the Godhead is certainly difficult, or rather impossible; but to read the existence of the Almighty Being in his works of nature, is not, I will dare to say, so difficult to the mind of a man possessed of common sense, and unfettered by prejudice, as to conceive artificial images to be possessed, at once, of the opposite natures of human and divine beings, which idolaters constantly ascribe to their idols;—strangely believing that things so *constructed* can be converted by ceremonies into *constructors* of the universe.

6thly. The learned gentleman objects to our introducing songs, although expressing only the peculiar tenets of monotheism, and says:

"But the holding of meetings, playing music, singing "songs, and dancing, which are ranked among car- "nal pleasures, are not ordained by scripture as "mental purification." The practice of dancing in divine worship, I agree, is not ordained by the scripture, and accordingly never was introduced in our worship; any mention of dancing in the Calcutta Gazette must, therefore, have proceeded from misinformation of the Editor. But respecting the propriety of introducing monotheistical songs in the divine worship, I beg leave to refer the gentleman to the text 114th and 115th of the 3d chapter of Yagnyavalca, who authorizes not only scriptural music in divine contemplation, but also the songs that are composed by the vulgar. It is also evident that any interesting idea is calculated to make more impression upon the mind, when conveyed in musical verses, than when delivered in the form of common conversation.

7thly The learned gentleman says: "All the Brah- "mins in this peninsula are studying the same "vedom as are read in the other parts of the country; "but I do not recollect to have read or heard of one "treating on astronomy, medicine, or arms: the first "is indeed an ongam of the Védam, but the two latter "are taught in separate Sastras." In answer to which I beg to be allowed to refer the gentleman to the following text of the Nervan: "The Véds, while talking "of planets, botany, austere duties, arms, rites, natu-

" ral consequences, and several other subjects, are pu-
" rified by the inculcation of the doctrines of the Su-
" preme Spirit." And also to the latter end of the Mahanervana agam.

From the perusal of these texts, I trust, he will be convinced that Védas not only treat of astronomy, medicine, and arms, but also of morality and natural philosophy, and that all arts and sciences that are treated of in other Sastras, were originally introduced by the Véds: see also Munoo, chapter 12, verses 97 and 98. I cannot of course be expected to be answerable for Bruhmans neglecting entirely the study of the scientific parts of the Véd, and putting in practice, and promulgating to the utmost of their power, that part of them which, treating of rites and festivals, is justly considered as the source of their wordly advantages and support of their alleged divinity.

8thly. I observe, that on the following statement in my Introduction to the Cenopunished, *viz.*, " should
" this explanation given by the Véd itself, as well as
" by its celebrated commentators Vyas, not be allowed
" to reconcile these passages which are seemingly at
" variance with each other, as those that declare the
" unity of the invisible Supreme Being, with others
" which describe a plurality of independent visible
" gods, the whole work must, I am afraid, not only be
" stripped of its authority, but looked upon as altoge-
" ther unintelligible," the learned gentleman has remarked that " To say the least of this passage, Ram
" Mohun Roy appears quite as willing to abandon as
" to defend the Scripture of his Religion."

In the foregoing paragraph, however, I did no more

than logically confine the case to two points, *viz.*, that the explanation of the Véd and of its commentators must either be admitted as sufficiently reconciling the apparent contradictions between different passages of the Véd, or must not be admitted. In the latter case, the Véd must necessarily be supposed to be inconsistent with itself, and therefore altogether unintelligible, which is directly contrary to the faith of Hindoos of every description; consequently they must admit that those explanations do sufficiently reconcile the seeming contradictions between the chapters of the Védas.

9thly. The learned gentleman says that "Their (the "attributes and incarnations) worship under various "representations, by means of consecrated objects, is "prescribed by the scripture to the human race, by "way of mental exercises," &c. I cannot admit that the worship of these attributes under various representations, by means of consecrated objects, has been prescribed by the Véd to the HUMAN RACE; as this kind of worship of consecrated objects is enjoined by the Sastra to those only who are incapable of raising their minds to the notion of an invisible Supreme Being. I have quoted several authorities for this assertion in my Preface to the Ishopanishad, and beg to repeat here one or two of them: "The vulgar look "for their God in water; men of more extended "knowledge in celestial bodies; the ignorant in wood, "bricks, and stones; but learned men in the universal "soul." "Thus corresponding to the nature of "different powers or qualities, numerous figures have "been invented for the benefit of those *who are* "*not possessed of sufficient understanding.*" Permit me in this instance to ask, whether every Mussulman in Turkey and Arabia, from the highest to the lowest, every Protestant Christian at least of Europe, and many followers of Cabeer and Nanuck, do worship God without the assistance of consecrated objects? If so, how can we suppose that the human race is not capable of adoring the Supreme Being without the puerile practice of having recourse to visible objects?

10thly. The learned gentleman is of opinion that the attributes of God exist distinctly from God; and he compares the relation between God and these attributes to that of a king to his ministers, as he says: "If a person be desirous to visit an earthly prince, "he ought to be introduced in the first instance by "his ministers," &c.; and "in like manner the Grace "of God ought to be obtained by the grace through "the worship of his attributes." This opinion, I am extremely sorry to find, is directly contrary to all the Védánt doctrines interpreted to us by the most revered Sankaracharjya, which are real adwaita or non-duality; they affirm that God has no second that may be possessed of eternal existence, either of the same nature with himself, or of a different nature from him, nor any second of that nature that might be called either his part or his *quality*. The 16th text of the 2d section of 3d chap.: "The Véd has declared the Supreme "Being to be mere understanding." The Véd says: "God is real existence, wisdom and eternity." The Véd very often calls the Supreme Existence by the epithets of Existent, Wise, and Eternal; and assigns as the reason for adopting such epithets, that the Véd in the first instance speaks of God according to human idea, which views quality separately from person, in order to facilitate our comprehension of objects. In case these attributes should be supposed, as the learned gentleman asserts, to be separate existences, it necessarily follows, that they must be either eternal or non-eternal. The former case, *viz.* the existence of a plurality of beings imbued like God himself with the property of eternal duration, strikes immediately at the root of all the doctrines relative to the unity of the Supreme Being contained in the Védánt. By the latter sentiment, namely, that the power and attributes of God are not eternal, we are led at once into the belief that the nature of God is susceptible of change, and consequently that He is not eternal, which makes no inconsiderable step towards atheism itself. These are the obvious and dangerous consequences, resulting from the learned gentleman's doctrine, that the attributes of the Supreme Being are distinct existences. I am quite at a loss to know how these attributes of the pure and perfect Supreme Being (as the learned gentleman declares them to exist really and separately, and not fictitiously and allegorically,) can be so sensual and destitute of morality, as the creating attribute or Brahma is said to be, by the Poorans; which represent him in one instance as attempting to commit a rape upon his own daughter. The protecting attribute, or Vishnu, is in another place affirmed to have fraudulently violated the chastity of Brinda, in order to kill her husband. Shiva, the destroying attribute, is said to have had a criminal attachment to Moheni, disregarding all ideas of decency. And a thousand similar examples must be familiar to every reader of the Poorans. I should be obliged by the learned gentleman's shewing how the contemplation of such circumstances, which are constantly related by the worshippers of these attributes, even in their sermons, can be instrumental towards the purification of the mind, conducive to morality, and productive of eternal beatitude. Besides, though the learned gentleman in this instance considers these attributes to be separate existences, yet in another place he seems to view them as parts of the Supreme Being, as he says: "If one part of the ocean be "adored, the ocean is adored." I am somewhat at a loss to understand how the learned gentleman proposes to reconcile this apparent contradiction. I must observe, however, in this place, that the comparison drawn between the relation of God and those attributes, and that of a king and his ministers, is totally inconsistent with the faith entertained by Hindoos of the present day; who, so far from considering these objects of worship as mere instruments by which they may arrive at the power of contemplating the God of Nature, regard them in the light of independent gods, to each of whom, however absurdly, they attribute almighty power, and a claim to worship, solely on his own account.

11thly. The learned gentleman is dissatisfied with the objection mentioned in my translation to worshipping these fictitious representations, and remarks, that "the objections to worshipping the attributes are "not satisfactorily stated by the author." I consequently repeat the following authorities, which I hope may answer my purpose. The following are the declarations of the Véd: "He, who worships any god "excepting the Supreme Being, and thinks that he "himself is distinct and inferior to that God, knows "nothing, and is considered as a domestic beast of "these gods." "A state even so high as that of "Brahma does not afford real bliss." "Adore God "alone." "None but the Supreme Being is to be "worshipped; nothing excepting him should be "adored by a wise man." I repeat also the following texts of the Védánt: "The declaration of the Véd, "that those that worship the celestial gods are the food "of such gods, is an allegorical expression, and only "means, that they are comforts to the celestial gods as "food to mankind; for he who has no faith in the "Supreme Being is rendered subject to these gods. "The Véd affirms the same."

And the revered Sankaracharjya has frequently declared the state of celestial gods to be that of demons, in the Bhasya of the Ishopanishad and of others.

To these authorities a thousand others might be added. But should the learned gentleman require some practical grounds for objecting to the idolatrous worship of the Hindoos, I can be at no loss to give him numberless instances, where the ceremonies that have been instituted under the pretext of honouring the all-perfect Author of Nature, are of a tendency utterly subversive of every moral principle.

I begin with Krishna as the most adored of all the incarnations, the number of whose devotees is exceedingly great. His worship is made to consist in the institution of his image or picture, accompanied by one or more females, and in the contemplation of his history and behaviour, such as his perpetration of murder upon a female of the name of Pootna; his compelling great number of married and unmarried women to stand before him denuded; his debauching them and several others, to the mortal affliction of their husbands and relations; his annoying them, by violating the laws of cleanliness and other facts of the same nature. The grossness of his worship does not find a limit here. His devotees very often personify (in the same manner as European actors upon stages do) him and his female companions, dancing with indecent gestures, and singing songs relative to his love and debaucheries. It is impossible to explain in language fit to meet the public eye, the mode in which Muhadéva, or the destroying attribute, is worshipped by the generality of the Hindoos: suffice it to say, that it is altogether congenial with the indecent nature of the image, under whose form he is most commonly adored.

The stories respecting him, which are read by his devotees in the Tuntras, are of a nature that, if told of any man, would be offensive to the ears of the most abandoned of either sex. In the worship of Kali, human sacrifices, the use of wine, criminal intercourse, and licentious songs, are included: the first of these practices has become generally extinct; but it is believed that there are parts of the country where human victims are still offered.

Debauchery, however, universally forms the principal part of the worship of her followers. Nigam and other Tantras may satisfy every reader of the horrible tenets of the worshippers of the two latter deities. The modes of worship of almost all the inferior deities are pretty much the same. Having so far explained the nature of worship adopted by Hindoos in general, for the propitiation of their allegorical attributes, in direct opposition to the mode of pure divine worship inculcated by the Védas, I cannot but entertain a strong hope that the learned gentleman, who ranks even monotheistical songs among carnal pleasures, and consequently rejects their admittance in worship, will no longer stand forward as an advocate for the worship of separate and independent attributes and incarnations.

12thly. The learned gentleman says, "that the Saviour," meaning Christ, "should be considered a personification of the mercy and kindness of God (I mean actual not allegorical personification)." From the little knowledge I had acquired of the tenets of Christians and those of anti-Christians, I thought there were only three prevailing opinions respecting the nature of Christ; *viz.* that he was considered by some as the expounder of the laws of God, and the mediator between God and man; by many to be one of the three mysterious persons of the Godhead; whilst others, such as the Jews, say that he was a mere man. But to consider Christ as a personification of the mercy of God is, if I mistake not, a new doctrine in Christianity, the discussion of which, however, has no connexion with the present subject. I however must observe that this opinion which the learned gentleman has formed of Christ being a personification of the mercy of God, is similar to that entertained by Mussulmans, for a period of upwards of a thousand years, respecting Mohummud, whom they call mercy of God upon all his creatures. The learned gentleman in the conclusion of his observations has left, as he says, the doctrines of pure allegory to me. It would have been more consistent with justice had he left pure allegory also to the Véds, which declare, "appellations "and figures of all kinds are innovations," and which have allegorically represented God in the figure of the universe: "Fire is his head, the sun and the moon are "his two eyes," &c.; and which have also represented all human internal qualities by different earthly objects; and also to Vyas, who has strictly followed the Véds in these figurative representations, and to Sankaracharjya, who also adopted the mode of allegory, in his Bhashya of the Védánt and of the Upanishadas.

A

SECOND DEFENCE

OF

THE MONOTHEISTICAL SYSTEM

OF

THE VEDS;

IN REPLY TO

AN APOLOGY FOR THE PRESENT STATE

OF

HINDOO WORSHIP.

CALCUTTA:
1817.

ADVERTISEMENT.

Two publications only have yet appeared with the professed object of defending Hindoo idolatry against the arguments which I have adduced from the Vedanta, and other sacred authorities, in proof of the erroneousness of that system. To the first, which appeared in a Madras Journal, my reply has been for some time before the public. The second, which is the object of the present answer, and is supposed to be the production of a learned Brahmun now residing in Calcutta, was printed both in Bengallee and in English; and I have therefore been under the necessity of preparing a reply in both of those languages. That which was intended for the perusal of my countrymen, issued from the press a few weeks ago. For my European readers I have thought it advisable to make some additional remarks to those contained in the Bengallee publication, which I hope will tend to make my arguments more clear and intelligible to them than a bare translation would do.

A

SECOND DEFENCE,

&c. &c.

THE learned Brahmun, in his defence of idolatry, thus begins: " Let it not be supposed that the following " treatise has been written with a view to refute the " doctrines of those assuming inventors and self-" interested moderns," &c. " It is solely with the inten-" tion of expressing the true meaning of these authori-" ties that this brief treatise has been composed;" and he thus concludes: " The Vedant chundrica, or lunar " light of the Vedant, has thus been made apparent, " and thus the glowworm's light has been eclipsed." It is very much to be feared that, from the perusal of this treatise, called the lunar light of the Vedant, but filled up with* satirical fables,† abusive expressions, and contradictory assertions, sometimes admitting monotheism, but at the same time blending with it and defending polytheism,‡ those foreign gentlemen, as well as those natives of this country who are not ac-

* P. 1, l. 26; p. 2, l. 17; p. 19 and 20, margin.

† P. 1; p. 3, l. 9; p. 8. l. 17; p. 38, l. 14; p. 48, l. 19, &c. &c.

‡ P. 13, l. 14.

quainted with the real tenets of the Vedant, might on a superficial view form a very unfavourable opinion of that theology, which, however, treats with perfect consistency of the unity and universality of the Supreme Being, and forbids, positively, treating with contempt or behaving ill towards any creature whatsoever.

As to the satire* and abuse, neither my education permits any return by means of similar language, nor does the system of my religion admit even a desire of unbecoming retaliation: situated as I am, I must *bear them tranquilly.*

Besides, a sect of people who are apt to make use of the most foul language, when they feel angry with their supposed deities,† cannot of course be expected, when irritated with contradiction, to pay due attention, unless checked by fear, to the propriety of the use of decent expressions, either in common conversation or in religious controversy.

The total sum of the arguments, set forth as far as page 13, of the translation of this treatise (however inconsistent they are with each other), seems intended to prove that faith in the Supreme Being, when united with moral works, leads men to eternal happiness.

This doctrine, I am happy to observe, strongly corroborates every assertion that I have made in my trans-

* Vide the "Apology," passim.

† As may be observed when at the annual festival of Juggunnath, the car in which he is conveyed happens to be impeded in its progress by any unseen obstacle In this case, the difficulty is supposed to be occasioned by the malicious opposition of that god, on whom the most gross abuse is liberally bestowed by his devotees.

lation; a few paragraphs of which I beg leave to repeat here for the satisfaction of my readers. In the abridgment of the Vedant, page 11th: "The Vedant shews "that moral principle is a part of the adoration of "God, *viz.* a command over passions and over the "external senses of the body, and good acts are de- "clared by the Ved to be indispensable in the mind's "approximation to God; they should therefore be "strictly taken care of, and attended to, both pre- "viously and subsequently to such approximation to "the Supreme Being; that is to say, we should not in- "dulge our evil propensities, but should endeavour to "have entire control over them: reliance on, and self- "resignation to the only true Being, with an aversion "to worldly considerations, are included in the good "acts above alluded to." In the introduction to the Ishopanished (page 5): "Under these impressions, "therefore, I have been impelled to lay before them "genuine translations of parts of their scriptures, which "inculcate not only the enlightened worship of One "God, but the purest principles of morality." But the learned Brahmin asserts, in two instances, among arguments above noticed, that the worship of a favoured deity and that of an image are also considered to be acts of morality. The absurdity of this assertion will be shown afterwards, in considering the subjects of idol-worship. To English readers, however, it may be proper to remark, that the Sungscrit word which signifies *works,* is not to be understood in the same sense as that which it implies in Christian theology, when works are opposed to faith. Christians understand by works, actions of *moral merit,* whereas Hindoos use the term in their theology only to denote religious rites and ceremonies prescribed by Hindoo lawgivers, which are often irreconcilable with the commonly received maxims of moral duty; as, for instance, the crime of suicide prescribed to widows by Ungeera, and to pilgrims at holy places by the Nursingh and Koorma Poorans. I do not, therefore, admit that works, taken in the latter sense (that is, the different religious acts prescribed by the Sastra to the different classes of Hindoos respectively) are necessary to attain divine faith, or that they are indispensable accompaniments of holy knowledge; for the Vedant in the chapter 3d, section 4, text 37th, positively declares that the true knowledge of God may be acquired without observing the rules and rites prescribed by the Sastra to each class of Hindoos; and also, examples are frequently found in the Ved, of persons, who, though they neglected the performance of religious rites and ceremonies, attained divine knowledge and absorption by control over their passions and senses, and by contemplation of the Ruler of the universe. Menu, the first and chief of all Hindoo lawgivers, confirms the same doctrines in describing the duties of laymen, in the texts 22d, 23d, and 24th of the 4th chapter of his work; and in the Bhashya, or commentaries on the Ishopanishad, and on the other Upanishads of the Veds, the illustrious Sankaracharjya declared the attainment of faith in God, and the adoration of the Supreme Being, to be entirely independent of Brahminical ceremonies; and the Ved affirms that "many "learned true believers never worshipped fire, nor any "celestial god through fire." The learned Brahmun, although he has acknowledged himself, in p. 9th, line 6th, of his treatise, that, "in the opinion of San- "karacharjya the attainment of absorption does not "depend on works of merit" (or, properly speaking, on religious rites), yet forgetting the obedience he has expressed to be due to the instruction* of that celebrated commentator, has immediately contradicted his opinion, when he says in p. 9, l. 9: "It has also been "ascertained that acts of merit (Brahminical rites) "must be performed previously to the attainment of "divine knowledge;" for, if divine knowledge were to be dependent on the observance of Brahminical rites, and absorption dependent on divine knowledge, it would follow necessarily that absorption would depend on Brahminical rites, which is directly contrary to the opinion of the commentator quoted by the learned Brahmun himself.

Moreover, the learned Brahmun at first states (p. 11, l. 12) that, "in the ancient writers we "read that a knowledge of Brahm, or holy knowledge, "is independent of acts" (religious rites); but he again contradicts this statement, and endeavours to explain it away (p. 11, l. 24): "Thus when the "Sastras state that absorption may be attained even "though the sacrificial fires be neglected, the praise of "that holy knowledge is intended, but *not* the depre- "ciation of meritorious acts" (Brahminical rites). Here he chooses to accuse his scripture, and ancient holy writers, of exaggerated and extravagant praise of holy knowledge, rather than that the least shock should be

* P. 3, l. 14.

given by their authority to the structure of paganism and idolatry. From this instance, the public may perceive how zealous the learned Brahmun and his brethren are, in respect to the preservation of their fertile estate of idolatry, when they are willing to sacrifice to it even their own scriptural authorities.

Upon a full perusal of the treatise, it appears that the arguments employed by the learned Brahmun have no other object than to support the weak system of idol-worship; inasmuch as he repeatedly declares, that the adoration of 330,000,000 deities, especially the principal ones, such as Siva, Vishnu, Kali, Gunesh, the Sun and others, through their several images, has been enjoined by the Shastras, and sanctioned by custom. I am not a little suprised to observe, that after having perused my Preface to the Ishopanishad in Bengali (of which during the last twelve months I have distributed nearly five hundred copies amongst all descriptions of Hindoos), the learned Brahmun has offered no objection to what I have therein asserted, relative to the reason assigned by the same Shastras, as well for the injunction to worship these figured beings, as for the general prevalence of idol-worship in this country.

In that work, I admitted that the worship of these deities was directed by the Shastra; but, at the same time, I proved by their own authority, that this was merely a concession made to the limited faculties of the vulgar, with the view of remedying, in some degree, the misfortune of their being incapable of comprehending and adopting the spiritual worship of the true God. Thus, in the aforesaid Preface, I remarked: "For they "(the Poorans, Tuntras, &c.) repeatedly declare "God to be one, and above the apprehension of the "external and internal senses. They indeed expressly "declare the divinity of many gods, and the mode of "their worship; but they reconcile those contradict- "ing assertions by affirming frequently, that the di- "rections to worship any celestial beings are only "applicable to those who are incapable of elevating "their minds to the idea of an invisible being." And, with the view to remove every doubt as to the correctness of my assertion, I at the same time quoted the most unquestionable authorities, a few of which I shall here repeat. "Thus corresponding to the natures of "different powers and qualities, numerous figures have "been invented for the benefit of those who are not "possessed of sufficient understanding." "The vulgar "look for their gods in water; men of more extended "knowledge, in celestial bodies; the ignorant, in wood, "bricks, and stones; but learned men in the universal "soul." "It is impossible for those who consider "pilgrimage as devotion, and believe that the divine "nature exists in the image, to look up to, communi- "cate with, to petition, and to serve true believers in "God."

Such indeed is the prevalent nature of truth, that when to dispute it is impossible, the learned Brahmun has not been always successful in concealing it, even when the admission is most fatal to his own argument. In p. 28, l. 34, he says: "But to those it is enjoined "who, from a *defective understanding*, do not perceive "that God exists in every thing, that they should "worship him through the medium of some created "object." In making this acknowledgment, the learned Brahmun has confirmed the correctness of all my assertions; though the evident conclusion is, that he and all his followers must either immediately give up all pretensions to understanding, or forsake idolatry.

In my former tract, I not only proved that the adoration of the Supreme Being in spirit was prescribed by the Ved to men of understanding, and the worship of the celestial bodies and their images to ignorant, but I also asserted, that the Ved actually prohibited the worship of any kind of figured beings by men of intellect and education. A few of the passages quoted by me in my former publications, on which this assertion rests, I also beg leave to repeat.

"He who worships any God except the Supreme "Being, and thinks that he himself is distinct and "inferior to that God, knows nothing, and is con-"sidered a domestic beast of these gods." "A state "even so high as that of Brahmâ, does not afford real "bliss." "Adore God alone. None but the Supreme "Being is to be worshipped; nothing excepting him "should be adored by a wise man." I repeat also the following text of the Vedant: "The declaration of the "Ved, that those that worship the celestial gods are "the food of such gods, is an allegorical expression, "and only means that they are comforts to the celes-"tial gods, as food to mankind; for he who has no "faith in the Supreme Being, is rendered subject to "these gods; the Ved affirms the same." No reply therefore is, I presume, required of me to the arguments adduced by the learned Brahmun in his treatise for idol-worship; except that I should offer some additional authorities, confirming exclusively the rational worship of the true God, and prohibiting the worship of the celestial figures and their images. I beg leave accordingly to quote, in the first instance, a few texts of the Ved: "Men may acquire eternal "beatitude, by obtaining a knowledge of the Supreme "Being alone; *there is no other way* to salvation."* —"To those that acquire a knowledge of Him, the "Ruler of the intellectual power, who is eternal "amidst the perishable universe, and is the source "of sensation among all animate existences, and who "alone assigns to so many objects their respective "purposes, everlasting beatitude is allotted; but not "to those who are not possessed of that knowledge."† And in the 4th, 5th, 6th, 7th, and 8th texts of the Cenopanishad, the Ved has, five times successively, denied the divinity of any specific being which men in general worship; and has affirmed the divinity of that Being solely, who is beyond description and comprehension, and out of the reach of the power of vision, and of the sense of hearing or of smelling. The most celebrated Sankaracharjya, in his commentary upon these texts, states that, lest people should suppose Vishnu, Mahadeba, Poven, Indra, or any other, to be a supreme spirit, the Ved in this passage disavows positively the divinity of all of them.—Again, the Ved says:‡ "Those that neglect the contemplation of the "Supreme Spirit, *either by devoting themselves solely to* "*the performance of the ceremonies of religion, or by* "*living destitute of religious ideas*, shall, after death,

* Sooctu. † Catha. ‡ Ishopanishad.

"assume the state of demons, *such as that of the celestial* "*gods, and of other created beings,* which are sur-"rounded with the darkness of ignorance." It will not, I hope, be supposed inconsistent with the subject in question to mention in this place in what manner the Vedant treats of these celestial gods, and how the Ved classes them among the other beings. The Vedant (c. 1st, s. 3d, t. 26th) has the following passage: "Vyas affirms that it is prescribed also to a celestial "gods and heavenly beings to attain a knowledge of "the Supreme Being, because a desire of absorption "is *equally* possible for them." And the Ved, in the Moonduc Upanishad, thus declares: "From Him, "who knows all things generally and particularly, and "who only by his omniscience *created the universe,* "Bruhmá, and whatever bears appellation, and figure "as well as food, all are produced." "From Him (the "Supreme Being) celestial gods* of many descriptions, "Siddha, or beings next to celestial gods, mankind, "beasts, birds, life, wheat, and barley, all are pro-"duced." In the Debee Mahatmya, a work which is as much in circulation among the Hindoos as their daily prayer-book,† (c. 1st, t. 66th) the creation of Vishnu, Brahma, and Mahadeva, is most distinctly affirmed.

Munoo, the best of all the commentators of the

* The Ved, having in the first instance personified all the attributes and powers of the Deity, and also the celestial bodies and natural elements, does, in conformity to this idea of personification, treat of them in the subsequent passages as if they were real beings, ascribing to them birth, animation, senses, and accidents, as well as liability to annihilation.

† Pooja Patal.

Veds, says (chap. 12th, text 85th): "Of all those "duties, answered Bhrigoo, the principal is to acquire "*from the Upanishad* a true knowledge of the one "Supreme Spirit, that is, the most exalted of all "sciences, because through that knowledge eternal "beatitude is obtained." And the same author, in the conclusion of his work on rites and ceremonies, thus directs (t. 92d, c. 12th): "Thus must the "chief of the twice-born, though he neglect the cere-"monial rites mentioned in the Shastras, be diligent "in attaining a knowledge of God, in controlling his "organs of sense, and in repeating the Ved." In the Coolarnuva, "absorption is not to be effected by "the studies of the Veds nor by the reading of other "Shastras: absorption is effected by a true knowledge "of the Supreme Being. O! Parbutee, except that "knowledge there is no other way to absorption." "Cast or religious order belonging to each sect, is not "calculated to be the cause of eternal beatitude, nor is "the study of Durshuns or any other Shastras, suffi-"cient to produce absorption: a knowledge of the "Supreme Spirit is alone the cause of eternal beati-"tude." Mahanervana: "He who believes that from "the highest state of Brahmá to the lowest state of a "straw, all are delusions, and that the one Supreme Spi-"rit is the only true being, attains beatitude." "Those "who believe that the divine nature exists in an image "made of earth, stone, metal, wood, or of other ma-"terials, reap only distress by their austerities; but "they cannot, without a knowledge of the Supreme "Spirit, acquire absorption."

I am really sorry to observe that, notwithstanding

these authorities and a thousand others of a similar nature, the learned Brahmun appears altogether unimpressed by the luminous manner in which they inculcate the sublime simple spiritual belief in, and worship of, one God, and that, on the contrary, he should manifest so much zeal in leading people into an idolatrous belief in the divinity of created and perishable beings.

Idolatry, as now practised by our countrymen, and which the learned Brahmun so zealously supports as conducive to morality, is not only rejected by the Shastras universally, but must also be looked upon with great horror by common sense, as leading directly to immorality and destructive of social comforts. For every Hindoo who devotes himself to this absurd worship, constructs for that purpose a couple of male and female idols, sometimes indecent in form, as representatives of his favourite deities; he is taught and enjoined from his infancy to contemplate and repeat the history of these, as well as of their fellow deities, though the actions ascribed to them be only a continued series of debauchery, sensuality, falsehood, ingratitude, breach of trust, and treachery to friends.* There can be but one opinion respecting the moral conduct to be expected of a person, who has been brought up with sentiments of reverence to such beings, who refreshes his memory relative to them almost every day, and who has been persuaded to believe, that a repetition of the *holy name* of one of these deities,* or a trifling present to his image or to his devotee, is sufficient, not only to purify and free him from all crimes whatsoever, but to procure to him future beatitude.

* Vide Note at the end.

As to the custom or practice to which the learned Brahmun so often refers in defence of idolatry, I have already, I presume, explained in the Preface of the Ishopanishad, the accidental circumstances which have caused idol-worship to flourish throughout the greater part of India; but, as the learned Brahmun has not condescended to notice any of my remarks on this subject, I beg leave to repeat here a part of them.

"Many learned Brahmuns are perfectly aware of the "absurdity of idolatry, and are well informed of the "nature of the pure mode of divine worship; but as in "the rites, ceremonies, and festivals of idolatry they find "the source of their comforts and fortune, they not "only never fail to protect idol-worship from all at-"tacks, but even advance and encourage it to the "utmost of their power, by keeping the knowledge of "their scriptures concealed from the rest of the people." And again: "It is, however, evident to every one pos-"sessed of common sense, that custom or fashion is "quite different from divine faith; the latter proceed-"ing from spiritual authorities and correct reasoning, "and the former being merely the fruit of vulgar ca-"price. What can justify a man, who believes in the "inspiration of his religious books, in neglecting the "direct authorities of the same works, and subjecting "himself entirely to custom and fashion, which are "liable to perpetual changes, and depend upon po-"pular whim? But it cannot be passed unnoticed, "that those who practise idolatry, and defend it under "the shield of custom, have been violating their cus-"toms almost every twenty years, for the sake of a "little convenience, or to promote their worldly advantages." Instances of this sort are mentioned in the preface of the Ishopanishad, and to those I beg leave to recal the attention of the learned Brahmun.

Every reader may observe, that the learned Brahmun in his treatise, written (as he says) on the doctrines of the Vedant, has generally neglected to quote any authority for his assertions; and when he cites the Ved or the Vedant (which he does sometimes) as his authority, he carefully omits to mention the text or part to which his assertion refers. The validity of theological controversy chiefly depends upon Scriptural authority, but when no authority is offered, the public may judge how far its credibility should extend. I shall, however, make a few remarks on the absurd and contradictory assertions with which the treatise abounds.

The learned Brahmun observes:* "But if the divine "essence itself, and not the energy be extolled, it will "be adored under the forms of Brahmá, Vishnu, and "Indra, and other male deities." And in other places, (p. 30, l. 27): "So by paying adoration to any material "object, animate or inanimate, the Supreme Being "himself is adored." If the truth of the latter assertion be admitted (namely, that God himself is adored by the adoration of any thing whatsoever), no mark of distinction between the adoration of any visible objects and male deities will exist; and the former assertion respecting the adoration of the Supreme Being through the male deities only, will appear an absurd restriction.

* P. 14, l. 14.

The learned Brahmun states (p. 19, l. 31), that, "If "you believe on the authority of the Scriptures, that "there is a Supreme Being, can you not believe that "he is united to matter?" A belief in God is by no means connected with a belief of his being united to matter: for those that have faith in the existence of the Almighty, and are endued with common sense, scruple not to confess their ignorance as to his nature or mode of existence, in regard to the point of his relation to matter, or to the properties of matter. How, therefore, can a belief in God's being united to matter, be inferred as a necessary consequence of a belief in his existence? The learned Brahmun again contradicts himself on this point, saying (p. 38, l. 19): "The divine "essence being supernatural and immaterial, a know-"ledge of it is to be acquired solely from revelations."

The learned Brahmun (in p. 18, l. 4): states that, "A quality cannot exist independently of its sub-"stance, but substance may exist independently of any "quality." Every one possessed of sensation is convinced, that a substance is as much dependent on the possession of some quality or qualities for its existence, as a quality on some substance. It is impossible even to imagine a substance divested of qualities. Despoil it as much as you please, that of magnitude must still remain. I therefore trust that the public will not suppose the above stated doctrines of the learned Brahmun to have been derived from those of the Vedant.

It is again stated (p. 21, l. 4) that, "In point of "fact, if you admit the existence of matter, as far as it "regards yourself, with its twenty-four accidents, as "confirmed by universal experience, you can easily "conceive that the same properties belong to the Supreme Being." It is easy enough for the learned Brahmun to conceive that the twenty-four properties which are peculiar to animals, and among which all sources of carnal pleasures are included, belong to his supposed deities; but it is difficult, or rather impossible, for a man untainted with idolatrous principles, to ascribe to God all such properties as he allows to exist in himself.

The learned Brahmun has drawn an analogy between the operation of the charms of the Veds, and that of magic; whereon he says (p. 18, l. 1): "Cannot the charms of the Veds operate as powerfully as those of magic, in producing effects where the cause is not present?" If the foundation of the Veds is held not to be stronger, as the learned Brahmun seems to consider it, than that of magic, I am afraid it will be found to rest on so slender a footing, that its doctrines will hardly be worth discussion.

In p. 24, l. 10, the learned Brahmun states that "The Vedant itself, in treating of the several deities, declares them to be possessed of forms, and their actions and enjoyments are all dependent on their corporeal nature." But (p. 21, l. 19) he says: "Because the male and female deities, whose being I contend for, are nothing more than accidents existing in the Supreme Being."

He thus at one time considers these deities as possessed of a corporeal nature, and at another declares them to be mere accidents in God; which are quite inconsistent with the attribute of corporeality. I am really at a loss to understand, how the learned Brahmun could admit so dark a contradiction into his "*Lunar* "*light of the Vedant.*"

The learned Brahmun (in p. 27, l. 6) thus assimilates the worship of the Supreme Being to that of an earthly king, saying "Let us drop the discourse con-"cerning a Supreme and Invisible Being; take an "earthly king. It is evident that, to serve him, there "must be the medium of materiality. Can service to "him be accomplished otherwise than by attendance "on his person, praising his qualities, or some similar "method?" Those who believe God to be an almighty, omniscient, and independent existence, which, pervading the universe, is deficient in nothing; and also know the feeble and dependent nature of earthly kings, as liable to sudden ruin, as harassed by incessant cares and wants, ought never, I presume, to assimilate the contemplation of the Almighty power with any corporeal service acceptable to an earthly king. But as by means of this analogy, the learned Brahmun and his brethen have successfully persuaded their followers to make, in imitation of presents and bribes offered to princes, pecuniary vows to these supposed deities, to which it would seem none but the learned Brahmun and his brethren have exclusive claim,—and as such analogy has thus become the source of their comforts and livelihood, I shall say no more upon so tender a subject.

He further observes (in p. 22, l. 27): "In reverting "to the subject, you affirm, that you admit the exis-"tence of matter in human beings, because it is evident "to your senses; but deny it with respect to God, be-"cause it is not evident to your senses," &c.; and, "If "this be your method of reasoning, it would appear "that your faith is confined to those objects only "which are evident to your senses." As far as my recollection goes with respect to the contents of my publications, both in the native language and in English, I believe I never denied the materiality of God, on the mere ground of its not being evident to our senses. The assertion which I quoted, or made use of in my former treatises, is, that the nature of the Godhead is beyond the comprehension of external and internal senses;* which, I presume, implies neither denial of the materiality of God, on the sole ground of his being invisible, nor the limitation of my faith merely to objects evident to the senses. For many things that far surpass the limits of our senses to perceive, or experience to teach, may yet be rendered credible, or even demonstrated by inferences drawn from our experience. Such as the mutual gravitation of the earth and moon towards each other, and of both to the sun; which facts cannot be perceived by any of our senses, but may be clearly demonstrated by reasoning drawn from our experience. Hence it appears, that a thing is justly denied, only, when found contrary to sense and reason, and not merely because it is not perceptible to the senses.

I have now to notice the friendly advice given me by the learned Brahmun (in p. 23, l. 16). "But at all the "events, divest yourself of the uneasy sensations you "profess to experience, at witnessing the worship paid "to idols, prepared at the expense and labour of

* The Preface to the Ishopanishad, p. 2, l. 9; p. 3, l. 2. The Abridgment of the Vedant, p. 1 and 2.

"another." In thanking him for his trouble in offering me this counsel, I must, however, beg the learned Brahmun to excuse me, while I acknowledge myself unable to follow it; and that for several reasons. 1st. A feeling for the misery and distress of his fellow creatures is, to every one not overpowered by selfish motives, I presume, rather natural than optional. 2dly. I, as one of their countrymen, and ranked in the most religious sect, of course participate in the disgrace and ridicule to which they have subjected themselves, in defiance of their scriptural authority, by the worship of idols, very often under the most shameful forms, accompanied with the foulest language, and most indecent hymns and gestures. 3dly. A sense of the duty which one man owes to another, compels me to exert my utmost endeavours to rescue them from imposition and servitude, and promote their comfort and happiness.

He farther observes (p. 30, l. 19): "In the like "manner, the King of Kings is served equally by those "worshippers who are acquainted with his real essence, "and by those who only recognize Him under the forms "of the deities; but in the future distribution of re-"wards a distinction will be made." As the learned Brahmun confesses, that the same reward is not promised to the worshippers of figured deities as to the adorers of the Supreme Being, it seems strange that he should persist in alleging that God is truly worshipped in the adoration of figured gods; for if the worship be in both cases the same, the reward bestowed by a just God must be the same to both; but the rewards are not the same to both, and therefore the worship of figured deities cannot be considered equal to the adoration of God.

In the same page (l. 7), he compares God to a mighty emperor; saying, "As a mighty emperor "travels through his kingdom in the garb of a peasant, "to effect the welfare of his subjects, so the King of "Kings pervades the universe, assuming a divine, or "even a human form, for the same benevolent pur-"pose." This comparison seems extremely objectionable, and the inference from it totally inadmissible. For a king being ignorant of things out of the reach of his sight, and liable to be deceived respecting the secrets and private opinions of his subjects, may sometimes be obliged to travel through his kingdom, to acquire a knowledge of their condition, and to promote their welfare personally. But there can be obviously no inducement for an omnipotent being, in whose omniscience also the learned Brahmun, I dare say, believes, to assume a form in order either to acquaint himself with the affairs of men, or to accomplish any benevolent design towards his creatures.

He again observes, that these figures and idols are representations of the true God, a sight of which serves, as he alleges, to bring that Being to his recollection (p. 30, l. 5): "They are as pictures, which recal "to the memory a dear and absent friend, or like the "worship of the moon, reflected in various waters."

This observation of the learned Brahmun, induces me to suppose that he must have formed a notion of Godhead quite strange and contemptible: for it is almost impossible for a man, who has a becoming idea of God's superiority to all creatures, to represent Him, as the Hindoos very often do, in a form so shameful, that a description of it is prohibited by common decency, or in a shape so ridiculous, as that piebald kite called Kshyemunkuree, and that of another bird called Neelkunth, or of jackals, &c. And it is equally difficult to believe that a rational being can make use of such objects to bring the All-perfect Almighty Power to his recollection.

He further says (p. 31, l. 32): " If any one assert " that the case is otherwise, that the deities, mankind, " the heavens, and other objects, have an existence in-" dependent of God, that faith in him is sufficient " without worship, that they (the deities) cannot meet " with reverence, how can that person affect to disbe-" lieve the doctrine of independent existence, or assert " that he is a believer in universality, or a follower of " the Vedant?" To acquit myself from such gross but unfounded accusation as that of my believing material existence to be independent of God, I repeat a few passages from the abridgment of the Vedant. (P. 6, l. 8): " Nothing bears true existence ex-" cepting God." Again in l. 9, " The existence of " whatever thing that appears to us, relies on the exis-" tence of God." Besides, there is not, I am confident, a single assertion in the whole of my publications, from which the learned Brahmun might justly infer that I believed in the independent existence of deities, mankind, the heavens, or other objects. The public, by an examination of these works, will be enabled to judge how far the learned Brahmun has ventured to brave public opinion, in the invention of arguments for the defence of idolatry.

He again says (p. 34, l. 28): " If, by the practice of " the prescribed forms in a church, a temple, or a

" mosque, God be worshipped, how can he be dis-" honoured by being worshipped under the form of an " image, however manufactured?" Those who contemplate God in a church or mosque, or elevate their minds to a notion of the Almighty Power in any other appropriated place, for the sake of good example, never pay divine homage to these places; but those that pretend to worship God under the form of an image, consider it to be possessed of divine nature, and at the same time, most inconsistently, as imbued with immoral principles. Moreover, the promoters of the worship of images, by promulgating anecdotes illustrative of the supposed divine power of particular idols, endeavour to excite the reverence of the people, and specially of pilgrims; who, under these superstitious ideas, are persuaded to propitiate them with large sacrifices of money, and sometimes even by that of their own lives. Having so far entered into this subject, the learned Brahmun will, I hope, be convinced of the impropriety of the analogy which he has drawn between a worship *within* a certain material object and a worship *of* a material object.

As to his question (p. 34, l. 32), " Is the sight of " the image unpleasing?" My answer must be affirmative. It is extremely natural that, to a mind whose purity is not corrupted by a degrading superstition, the sight of images which are often of the most hideous or indecent description, and which must therefore excite disgust in the minds of the spectator, should be unpleasing. A visit to Calighaut,* or Barahnagur,† which

* The temple of Kali.

† Where there are twelve temples dedicated to Siva.

are only distant four miles from Calcutta, will sufficiently convince the reader of the unpleasant nature of their beloved images. He again asks in the same page, (l. 33): "Will a beloved friend be treated with disre-"spect by being seated on a chair, when he arrives in "your house, or by being presented with fragrant "flowers and other offerings?" To which I shall say no; but at the same time I must assert that a friend worthy of reverence would not, we may be sure, be at all pleased at being exhibited sometimes in a form,* the bare mention of which would be considered as a gross insult to the decorous feelings of the public; and sometimes in the shape of a monkey,† fish,‡ hog,§ or elephant,|| or at being represented as destitute of every virtue, and altogether abandoned. Nor would he believe his host to be possessed of common sense, who, as a token of regard, would altogether neglect his guest, to go and lay fruits and flowers before his picture.

It is said (p. 39, l. 23): "In the accounts of ancient "Greece we meet with the worship of idols, and the "practice of austerities; but these acts have been "contemned by the more enlightened moderns." I am really glad to observe that the learned Brahmun, more liberally and plainly than could be expected, confesses that idolatry will be totally contemned as soon as the understanding is improved. I, however, beg leave to remark on this instance, that though the idolatry practised by the Greeks and Romans was certainly just

* Under which Siva is adored. † Hunooman.

‡ The first incarnation of Vishnu.

§ The third incarnation of ditto. || Gunesh.

as impure, absurd, and puerile as that of the present Hindoos, yet the former was by no means so destructive of the comforts of life, or injurious to the texture of society, as the latter. The present Hindoo idolatry being made to consist in following certain modes and restraints of diet (which according to the authorities of the Mahabharut and other histories were never observed by their forefathers), has subjected its unfortunate votaries to entire separation from the rest of the world, and also from each other, and to constant inconveniences and distress.

A Hindoo, for instance, who affects particular purity, * cannot even partake of food dressed by his own brother, when invited to his house; and if touched by him while eating, he must throw away the remaining part of his meal. In fact, owing to the observance of such peculiar idolatry, directly contrary to the authorities of their scripture, they hardly deserve the name of social beings.

The learned Brahmun further says (p. 23, l. 3): "If you affirm that you are not an infidel, but that "your arguments are in conformity with those of the "philsophers who were ignorant of the Veds," &c. A remark of this kind cannot, I am sure, be considered as at all applicable to a person, who has subjected himself to this writer's remarks only by translating and publishing the principal parts of the Ved, and by vindicating the Vedant theology; and who never advanced on religious controversy any argument which was not founded upon the authorities of the Veds and

* A person of this description is distinguished by the name of Swayung pak, one who is his own cook.

their celebrated commentators. It is, however, remarkable that, although the learned Brahmun and his brethren frequently quote the name of the Veds and other Shastras, both in writing and in verbal discussion, they pay little or no attention in practice to their precepts, even in the points of the most important nature, a few of which I beg leave to notice here. 1st, The adoration of the invisible Supreme Being, although exclusively prescribed by the Upanishads, or the principal parts of the Veds, and also by the Vedant, has been totally neglected, and even discountenanced, by the learned Brahmun and his followers; the idol-worship, which those authorities permit only to the ignorant, having been substituted for that pure worship. 2dly, Ungeera and Vishnu, and also the modern Rughonundun, authorize a widow to burn herself voluntarily along with the corpse of her husband: but modern Brahmuns, in direct opposition to their authority, allow her relations to bind the mournful and infatuated widow to the funeral pile with ropes and bamboos, as soon as she has expressed a wish to perform the dreadful funeral sacrifice, to which the Brahmuns lend a ready assistance. 3dly, Although an acceptance of money or of a present in the marriage contract of a daughter is most strictly prohibited by the Veds and by Munoo (text 98 and 100 of chap. 9), yet the sale of female children under pretence of marriage is practised by nearly two-thirds of the Brahmuns of Bengal and Tirhoot, as well as by their followers generally.

4thly. Yagnyubulkya has authorized the second marriage of a man, while his former wife is living; but only under certain circumstances of misconduct or misfortune in the latter, such as the vice of drinking wine, of deception, of extravagance, of using disagreeable language, or shewing manifest dislike towards her husband; long protracted and incurable illness, barrenness, or producing only female offspring. In defiance, however, of this restraint, some of them marry thirty or forty women, either for the sake of money got with them at marriage, or to gratify brutal inclinations. Madhosingh, the late Rajah of Tirhoot, through compassion towards that helpless sex, limited, I am told, within these thirty or forty years, the Brahmuns of that district to four wives only. This regulation, although falling short both of the written law and of that of reason, tends to alleviate in some measure the misery to which women were before exposed, as well as to diminish in some degree domestic strife and disturbance.

5thly. According to the authority of Munoo (text 155, chap. 2d), respect and distinction are due to a Brahmun, merely in proportion to his knowledge; but on the contrary amongst modern Hindoos, honour is paid exclusively to certain families of Brahmuns, such as the Koolins, &c., however void of knowledge and principle they may be. This departure from law and justice was made by the authority of a native prince of Bengal, named Bullalsen, within the last three or four hundred years. And this innovation may perhaps be considered as the chief source of that decay of learning and virtue, which, I am sorry to say, may be at present observed. For wherever respectability is confined to birth only, acquisition of knowledge, and the practice of morality, in that country, must rapidly decline.

The learned Brahmun objects to the term *indescribable*, although universally assigned to the Supreme Being by the Ved, and by the Vedant theology, saying (p. 37, l. 20), "it is a wonderful interpretation of "the Vedant to say that God is indescribable, although "existing, unless indeed he be looked upon as the "production of magic; as existing in one sense, and "non-existent in another." And again (l. 14), "he, "therefore, who asserts that the Supreme Being is "indescribable and at the same time existing, must "conceive that He, like the world, is mutable," &c. In answer to which I beg to refer the learned Brahmun to the 11th text of the 3d Brahmun of the 4th chapter of the Brehdarunyuc, the principal part of the Ujoor Ved, as commented upon by the celebrated Sunkaracharjya: "The Ved having so far described God, by "various absolute* and relative epithets,† was con-"vinced of its incapability of giving a real description "of the nature of the Godhead: language can convey "a notion of things only either by the appellations by "which they are already known, or by describing "their figure, accidents, genus, and properties; but "God has none of these physical circumstances: the "Ved therefore attempted to explain him in negative "terms;" (that is, by declaring that whatever thing may be perceived by the mental faculties, or the external senses, is not God.) "The Ved's ascribing to God "attributes of eternity, wisdom, truth, &c., shews that "it can explain him only by ascribing those attributes, "and applying those epithets, that are held by man

* As eternal, true, and intelligent.

† As creator, preserver, and destroyer.

"in the highest estimation, without intending to "assert the adequacy of such description. He is the "only true existence amidst all dependent existences, "and the true source of our senses." Also in the text 3d of the Cenopanishad: "Hence no vision can "approach him; no language can describe him; no in- "tellectual power can compass or determine him. We "know nothing of how the Supreme Being should be "explained: He is beyond nature, which is above com- "prehension: our ancient *spiritual parents* have thus "explained Him to us." It cannot, however, be inferred, from our acknowledged ignorance of the nature and attributes of the Supreme Being, that we are equally ignorant as to His existence. The wonderful structure and growth of even so trifling an object as a leaf of a tree, affords proof of an Almighty Superintendent of the universe; and even the physical world affords numerous instances of things whose existence is quite evident to our senses, but of whose nature we can form no conception; such as the causes of the sensations of heat and vision.

The learned Brahmun attempts to prove the impossibility of an adoration of the Deity, saying (p. 33, l. 15): "That which cannot be conceived, cannot be wor- "shipped." Should the learned Brahmun consider a full conception of the nature, essence, or qualities of the Supreme Being, or a physical picture truly representing the Almighty power, with offerings of flowers, leaves, and viands, as essential to adoration, I agree with the learned Brahmun with respect to the impossibility of the worship of God. But, should adoration imply only the elevation of the mind to the conviction of the existence of the Omnipresent Deity, as testified by His wise and wonderful works, and continual contemplation of His power as so displayed; together with a constant sense of the gratitude which we naturally owe Him, for our existence, sensation, and comfort,—I never will hesitate to assert, that His adoration is not only possible, and practicable, but even incumbent upon every rational creature. For further explanation, I refer the learned Brahmun to the text 47, sect. 4, chap. 3, of the Vedant.

To his question,* "what are you yourselves?" I suppose I may safely reply for myself, that I am a poor dependent creature;—subject, in common with others, to momentary changes, and liable to sudden destruction.

At p. 45, l. 30, the learned Brahmun, if I rightly understand his object, means to insinuate, that I have adopted the doctrines of those who deny the responsibility of man as a moral agent. I am quite at a loss to conceive from what part of my writings this inference has been drawn, as I have not only never entertained such opinions myself, but have taken pains to explain the passage in the Ved on which this false doctrine is founded. In page 93 of the Preface to the Ishopanishad, I have said that, "the Vedant by declaring that "God is every where, and every thing is in God, means "that nothing is absent from God, and that nothing "bears real existence except by the volition of God." And again, in the same page I quoted the example of the most revered teachers of the Vedant doctrine, who,

* P. 47, l. 4

" although they declared their faith in the Omnipresent " God, according to the doctrines of the Vedant, as- " signed to every creature the particular character and " respect he was entitled to."

I omitted to notice the strange mode of argument which the learned Brahmun (at p. 29) has adopted in defence of idolatry. After acknowledging that the least deficiency in judgment renders man incapable of looking up to an Omnipresent Supreme Being, whereby he mistakes a created object for the great Creator, he insinuates that an erroneous notion in this respect is as likely to lead to eternal happiness, as a knowledge of truth. At l. 5, he says: " And although " a person through deficiency in judgment, should be " unable to discover the real nature of a thing, does " it follow, that his error will prevent the natural effect " from appearing? When a man in a dream sees a " tiger, is he not in as much alarm as if he saw it in " reality?"

This mode of claiming for idol-worship a value equal to that of pure religion, which it can never be admitted to possess, may have succeeded in retaining some of his followers in the delusive dream, from which he is so anxious that they should not be awoke. But some of them have, I know, begun to inquire into the truth of those notions in which they have been instructed; and these are not likely to mistake for true, the false analogy that is in the above passage attempted to be drawn; nor will they believe that, however powerful may be the influence of imagination, even under false impressions, future happiness, which depends on God alone, can ever be ranked amongst its effects. Such enquirers will, I hope, at last become sensible that the system of *dreaming* recommended by the learned Brahmun, however essential to the interests of himself and of his cast, can bring to them no advantage, either substantial or eternal.

As instances of the erroneous confidence which is placed in the repetition of the name of a god to effect purification from sins, noticed by me in p. 168, I may quote the following passages.

He who pronounces "Doorga" (the name of the goddess), though he constantly practise adultery, plunder others of their property, or commit the most heinous crimes, is freed from all sins.*

A person pronouncing loudly, "reverence to Huri," even involuntarily, in the state of falling down, of slipping, of labouring under illness, or of sneezing, purifies himself from the foulest crimes.†

He who contemplates the Ganges, while walking, sitting, sleeping, thinking of other things, awake, eating, breathing, and conversing, is delivered from sins.‡

The circumstances alluded to in p. 168 of this treatise, relative to the wicked conduct of their supposed deities, are perfectly familiar to every individual Hindoo. But those Europeans who are not acquainted with the particulars related of them, may perhaps feel a wish to be in possession of them. I therefore, with a view to gratify their curiosity and to vindicate my assertion, beg to be allowed to mention a few instances in point, with the authorities on which they rest. As I have already noticed the debauchery of Krishna, and his

* Vide Doorga nám Mahatmyu.

† Vide Bhágavut.

‡ Vide Mahabharuth.

gross sensuality, and that of his fellow deities, such as Siva and Bruhma, in the 147th, 148th, and 150th page of my reply to the observations of Sunkarasastri, instead of repeating them here, I refer my readers to that reply, and also to the tenth division of the Bhaguvut, to the Hurybungsu or last division of the Mahabharuth, and to the Negums, as well as to the several Agums, which give a detailed account of their lewdness and debauchery. As to falsehood, their favourite deity Krishna is more conspicuous than the rest. Jurra-Sundh, a powerful prince of Behar, having heard of the melancholy murder of his son-in-law perpetrated by Krishna, harassed, and at last drove him out of the place of his nativity (Muthoora) by frequent military expeditions. Krishna, in revenge, resolved to deprive that prince of his life by fraud, and in a most unjustifiable manner. To accomplish his object, he and his two cousins, Bheema and Urjoona, declared themselves to be Brahmuns, and in that disguise entered his palace; where finding him weakened by a religious fast, and surrounded only by his family and priests, they challenged him to fight a duel. He accordingly fought Bheema, the strongest of the three; who conquered and put him to death.—*Vide Subha Purba or second Book of the Maha-Bharuth.* Krishna again persuaded Joodhisthir, his cousin, to give false evidence in order to accomplish the murder of Dron their spiritual father.—*Vide Dron Purba, or seventh Book of the Maha-Bharuth.*

Vishnu and others combined in a conspiracy against Buli, a mighty emperor; but finding his power irresistible, that deity was determined to ruin him by stratagem, and for that purpose appeared to him in the shape of a dwarf, begging alms. Notwithstanding Buli was warned of the intention of Vishnu, yet, impressed with a high sense of generosity, he could not refuse a boon to a beggar; that grateful deity in return not only deprived him of his whole empire, which he put himself in possession of by virtue of the boon of Buli, but also inflicted on him the disgrace of bondage and confinement in Patal.—*Vide latter part of the Hurri Bungs, or last book of the Maha-Bharuth.*

When the battle of Coorookshetru was decided by the fatal destruction of Doorjodhun, the remaining part of the army of his rival Yooddhisthir, returned to the camp to rest during the night, under the personal care and protection of Mahadeva. That deity having, however, been cajoled by the flattery offered him by Uswathama, one of the friends of the unfortunate Doorjodhun, not only allowed him to destroy the whole army that was asleep under the confidence of his protection, but even assisted him with his sword to accomplish his bloody purpose.—*Vide Sousuptik Purb, or eleventh book of the Maha-Bharuth.*

When the Ussoors, at the churning of the ocean, gave the pitcher of *the water of immortality* in charge to Vishnu, he betrayed his trust by delivering it to their step-brothers and enemies, the celestial gods.—*Vide first book, or ádi Purb of the Maha-Bharuth.*

Instances like these might be multiplied beyond number: and crimes of a much deeper dye might easily be added to the list, were I not unwilling to stain these pages by making them the vehicle of such stories of immorality and vice. May God speedily purify the minds of my countrymen from the corruptness which such tales are too apt to produce; and lead their hearts to that pure morality, which is inseparable from the true worship of Him!

AN APOLOGY

FOR THE

PURSUIT OF FINAL BEATITUDE,

INDEPENDENTLY OF

BRAHMUNICAL OBSERVANCES.

CALCUTTA:
1820.

AN APOLOGY

FOR THE

PURSUIT OF FINAL BEATITUDE.

SOOBRAHMUNYU SHASTREE, a diligent observer of Brahmunical tenets, wishing to prove that those Brahmuns who do not study the Veds with their subordinate sciences, are degraded from the rank of Brahmunism, prepared and offered an Essay on that subject to the Brahmuns of the province of Bengal, who are generally deficient in those studies. In this, he has advanced three assertions: which, however, have no tendency to establish his position. He alleges 1st, that, "to a "person not acquainted with the Veds, neither temporary heavenly enjoyments, nor eternal beatitude, "can be allotted." 2dly, that, "he only who has "studied the Veds is authorized to seek the knowledge "of God;" and 3dly, that "men must perform without omission all the rites and duties prescribed in "the Veds and Smritis before acquiring a thorough "knowledge of God." On these positions he attempts to establish, that the performance of the duties and rites prescribed by the Shastrus for each class according to their religious order, such as the studies of the Veds and the offering of sacrifices, &c., is absolutely necessary towards the acquisition of a knowledge of

God. We consequently take upon ourselves to offer in our own defence the following remarks, in answer to those assertions.

We admit that it is proper in men to observe the dutes and rites prescribed by the Shastru for each class according to their religious order, in acquiring knowledge respecting God, such observance being conducive to that acquisition; an admission which is not inconsistent with the authorities of the Veds and other Shastrus. But we can by no means admit the necessity of observing those duties and rites as indispensable steps towards attaining divine knowledge, which the learned Shastree pronounces them to be; for the great Vyas, in his work of the Vedant Durshun, or the explanation of the spiritual parts of the Veds, justifies the attainment of the knowledge of God, even by those who never practise the prescribed duties and rites, as appears from the following two passages of Vyas in the same Durshun. "Unturachapitoo tuddrishteh,"— "Upichu shmuryute." The celebrated Shunkur Acharyu thus comments upon those two texts: "As "to the question, Whether such men as have not the "sacred fire, or are afflicted with poverty, who profess "no religious order whatsoever, and who do not belong "to any cast, are authorized to seek divine knowledge "or not? On a superficial view, it appears, that they "are not permitted to make such attainments, as the "duties prescribed for each class are declared to lead "to divine knowledge, and to those duties they are "altogether strangers. Such doubt having arisen, the "great Vyas thus decides: Even a person who pro- "fesses no religious order, is permitted to acquire a

" knowledge of God; for it is found in the Veds that " Rüekyu, Bachuknuvee, and others, who, like them, " did not belong to any class, obtained divine know- " ledge. It is also mentioned in the sacred tradition, " that Sumvurtu and others, living naked and totally " independent of the world, who practised no pre- " scribed duties, assumed the rank of the highest " devotees." Besides the texts of the Ved, such as " Tuyorhu Müetreyee Bruhmubadinee," &c. and " Atma va Ure," &c. show that Müetreyee and others, who, being women, had not the option of studying the Ved, were, notwithstanding, qualified to acquire divine knowledge; and in the Smriti as well as in the Commentary of the celebrated Shunkur Acharyu, Soolubha and other women are styled knowers of the Supreme Being. Also Bidoor, Dhurmubyadhu, and others of the fourth class, attained the knowledge of God without having an opportunity of studying the Veds. All this we find in the sacred traditions: hence those who have a thorough knowledge of the Veds and Smriti, can pay no deference to the opinion maintained by the learned Shastree, that those only who have studied the Veds are qualified to acquire the knowledge of God. Moreover, to remove all doubt as to Soodrus and others being capable of attaining Divine knowledge without the assistance of the Veds, the celebrated Commentator, in illustrating the text " Sruvunadhyun," &c., asserts, that " the authority of the Smriti, stating that ' to all " ' the four classes preaching should be offered,' &c. " shews that to the sacred traditions, and to the Poo- " rans, and also to the Agums, all the four classes have " equally access." Thus establishin that the sacred traditions, Poorans, and Agum without distinction, can impart divine knowledge to mankind at large. From the decided opinion of Vyas, and from the precedents given by the Veds and sacred traditions, and also from the conclusive verdict of the most revered Commentator, those who entertain respect for those authorities, will not admit the studies of the Veds and other duties required of each class to be the only means of acquiring knowledge of God. Hence the sacred tradition, stating that a person, by studying the Geeta alone, had acquired final beatitude, stands unshaken; and also the positive declaration of the great Muhadevu with regard to the authentic and well-accepted Agum Shastrus, as being the means of imparting divine knowledge to those who study them, will not be treated as inconsequential. If the spiritual parts of the Veds can enable men to acquire salvation by teaching them the true and eternal existence of God, and the false and perishable being of the universe, and inducing them to hear and constantly reflect on those doctrines, it is consistent with reason to admit, that the Smriti, and Agum, and other works, inculcating the same doctrines, afford means of attaining final beatitude. What should we say more?

TRANSLATION

OF A

CONFERENCE

BETWEEN

AN ADVOCATE FOR, AND AN OPPONENT OF,

THE PRACTICE OF

BURNING WIDOWS ALIVE;

FROM THE

ORIGINAL BUNGLA.

ADVERTISEMENT.

The little tract, of which the following is a literal translation, originally written in Bungla, has been for several weeks past in extensive circulation in those parts of the country where the practice of Widows burning themselves on the pile of their Husbands is most prevalent. An idea that the arguments it contains might tend to alter the notions that some European Gentlemen entertain on this subject, has induced the Writer to lay it before the British Public also in its present dress.

Nov. 30, 1818.

CONFERENCE

BETWEEN

AN ADVOCATE FOR, AND AN OPPONENT OF,

THE PRACTICE OF

BURNING WIDOWS ALIVE.

Advocate.—I AM surprised that you endeavour to oppose the practice of Concremation and Postcremation of Widows,* as long observed in this country.

Opponent.—Those who have no reliance on the Shastru, and those who take delight in the self-destruction of women, may well wonder that we should oppose that suicide which is forbidden by all the Shastrus, and by every race of men.

Advocate.—You have made an improper assertion, in alleging that Concremation and Postcremation are forbidden by the Shastrus. Hear what Unggira and other saints have said on this subject:

" That woman who, on the death of her husband,
" ascends the burning pile with him, is exalted to hea-
" ven, as equal to Uroondhooti.

" She who follows her husband to another world,

* When a widow is absent from her husband at the time of his death, she may in certain cases burn herself along with some relick representing the deceased. This practice is called Unoomurun or Postcremation.

" shall dwell in a region of joy for so many years as " there are hairs in the human body, or thirty-five " millions.

" As a serpent-catcher forcibly draws a snake from " his hole, thus raising her husband by her power, she " enjoys delight along with him.

" The woman who follows her husband expiates the " sins of three races; her father's line, her mother's line, " and the family of him to whom she was given a virgin.

" There possessing her husband as her chiefest good, " herself the best of women, enjoying the highest de- " lights, she partakes of bliss with her husband as long " as fourteen Indrus reign.

" Even though the man had slain a Brahmun, or re- " turned evil for good, or killed an intimate friend, the " woman expiates those crimes.

" There is no other way known for a virtuous woman " except ascending the pile of her husband. It should " be understood that there is no other duty whatever " after the death of her husband."

Hear also what Vyas has written in the parable of the pigeon:

" A pigeon devoted to her husband, after his death " entered the flames, and ascending to heaven, she " there found her husband."

And hear Hareet's words:

" As long as a woman shall not burn herself after her " husband's death, she shall be subject to transmigra- " tion in a female form."

Hear too what Vishnoo the saint says:

" After the death of her husband a wife must live as " an ascetic, or ascend his pile."

Now hear the words of the Bruhmu Pooran on the subject of Postcremation:

"If her lord die in another country, let the faithful "wife place his sandals on her breast, and pure enter "the fire."

The faithful widow is declared no suicide by this text of the Rig Ved: "When three days of impurity "are gone she obtains obsequies." Gotum says:

"To a Brahmunee after the death of her husband, "Postcremation is not permitted. But to women of the "other classes it is esteemed a chief duty."

"Living let her benefit her husband; dying she "commits suicide."

"The woman of the Brahmun tribe that follows her "dead husband cannot, on account of her self-de-"struction, convey either herself or her husband to "heaven."

Concremation and Postcremation being thus established by the words of many sacred lawgivers, how can you say they are forbidden by the Shastrus, and desire to prevent their practice?

Opponent.—All those passages you have quoted are indeed sacred law; and it is clear from those authorities, that if women perform Concremation or Postcremation, they will enjoy heaven for a considerable time. But attend to what Munoo and others say respecting the duty of widows: "Let her emaciate her "body, by living voluntarily on pure flowers, roots, "and fruits, but let her not, when her lord is deceased, "even pronounce the name of another man."

"Let her continue till death forgiving all injuries, "performing harsh duties, avoiding every sensual plea-

"sure, and cheerfully practising the incomparable rules "of virtue which have been followed by such women as "were devoted to one only husband."

Here Munoo directs, that after the death of her husband, the widow should pass her whole life as an ascetic. Therefore, the laws given by Unggira and the others whom you have quoted, being contrary to the law of Munoo, cannot be accepted; because the Ved declares, "whatever Munoo has said is wholesome;" and Virhusputi, "whatever law is contrary to the law "of Munoo is not commendable." The Ved especially declares, "by living in the practice of regular and "occasional duties the mind may be purified. There-"after by hearing, reflecting, and constantly meditat-"ing on the Supreme Being, absorption in Bruhmu "may be attained. Therefore from a desire during "life of future fruition, life ought not to be destroyed." Munoo, Yagnyuvulkyu, and others, have then, in their respective codes of laws, prescribed to widows the duties of ascetics only. By this passage of the Ved, therefore, and the authority of Munoo and others, the words you have quoted from Unggira and the rest are set aside; for by the express declaration of the former, widows after the death of their husbands may, by living as ascetics, obtain absorption.

Advocate.—What you have said respecting the laws of Unggira and others, that recommended the practice of Concremation and Postcremation, we do not admit: because, though a practice has not been recommended by Munoo, yet, if directed by other lawgivers, it should not on that account be considered as contrary to the law of Munoo. For instance, Munoo directs the performance of Sundhya, but says nothing of calling aloud on the name of Huri; yet Vyas prescribes calling on the name of Huri. The words of Vyas do not contradict those of Munoo. The same should be understood in the present instance. Munoo has commended widows to live as ascetics; Vishnoo and other saints direct that they should either live as ascetics or follow their husbands. Therefore the law of Munoo may be considered to be applicable as an alternative.

Opponent.—The analogy you have drawn betwixt the practice of Sundhya and invoking Huri, and that of Concremation and Postcremation, does not hold. For, in the course of the day the performance of Sundhya, at the prescribed time, does not prevent one from invoking Huri at another period; and, on the other hand, the invocation of Huri need not interfere with the performance of Sundhya. In this case, the direction of one practice is not inconsistent with that of the other. But in the case of living as an ascetic or undergoing Concremation, the performance of the one is incompatible with the observance of the other. *Scil.* Spending one's whole life as an ascetic after the death of a husband, is incompatible with immediate Concremation as directed by Unggira and others; and, *vice versa*, Concremation, as directed by Unggira and others, is inconsistent with living as an ascetic, in order to attain absorption. Therefore those two authorities are obviously contradictory of each other. More especially as Unggira, by declaring that "there is no "other way known for a virtuous woman except "ascending the pile of her husband," has made Concremation an indispensable duty. And Hareet also, in his code, by denouncing evil consequences, in his declaration, that "as long as a woman shall not burn "herself after the death of her husband, she shall be "subject to transmigration in a female form," has made this duty absolute. Therefore all those passages are in every respect contradictory to the law of Munoo and others.

Advocate.—When Unggira says that there is no other way for a widow except Concremation, and when Hareet says that the omission of it is a fault, we reconcile their words with those of Munoo, by considering them as used merely for the purpose of exalting the merit of Concremation, but not as prescribing this as an indispensable duty. All these expressions, moreover, convey a promise of reward for Concremation, and thence it appears that Concremation is only optional.

Opponent.—If, in order to reconcile them with the text of Munoo, you set down the words of Unggira and Hareet, that make the duty incumbent, as meant only to convey an exaggerated praise of Concremation, why do you not also reconcile the rest of the words of Unggira, Hareet, and others, with those in which Munoo prescribes to the widow the practice of living as an ascetic as her absolute duty? And why do you not keep aloof from witnessing the destruction of females, instead of tempting them with the inducement of future fruition? Moreover, in the text already quoted, self-destruction with the view of reward is expressly prohibited.

Advocate.—What you have quoted from Munoo and Yagnyavulkyu and the text of the Ved is admitted. But how can you set aside the following text of the Rig Ved on the subject of Concremation? "O fire! let "these women, with bodies anointed with clarified "butter, eyes coloured with collyrium, and void of "tears, enter thee, the parent of water, that they may "not be separated from their husbands, but may be, in "unison with excellent husbands, themselves sinless "and jewels amongst women."

Opponent.—This text of the Ved, and the former passages from Hareet and the rest whom you have quoted, all praise the practice of Concremation as leading to fruition, and are addressed to those who are occupied by sensual desires; and you cannot but admit that to follow these practices is only optional. In repeating the Sunkulpyu of Concremation, the desire of future fruition is declared as the object. The text therefore of the Ved which we have quoted, offering no gratifications, supersedes, in every respect, that which you have adduced, as well as all the words of Unggira and the rest. In proof we quote the text of the Kuthopunishut: "Faith in God which leads to absorption "is one thing; and rites which have future fruition for "their object, another. Each of these, producing dif-"ferent consequences, holds out to man inducements "to follow it. The man, who of these two chooses "faith, is blessed; and he, who for the sake of reward "practises rites, is dashed away from the enjoyment of "eternal beatitude." Also the Moonduk Opunishut: "Rites, of which there are eighteen members, are all "perishable: he who considers them as the source of "blessing shall undergo repeated transmigrations; "and all those fools who, immersed in the foolish "practice of rites, consider themselves to be wise and "learned, are repeatedly subjected to birth, disease, "death, and other pains. When one blind man is "guided by another, both subject themselves on their "way to all kinds of distress."

It is asserted in the Bhugvut Geeta, the essence of all the Smritis, Poorans, and Itihases, that, "all those "ignorant persons who attach themselves to the words "of the Veds that convey promises of fruition, consider "those falsely alluring passages as leading to real hap-"piness; and say, that besides them there is no other "reality. Agitated in their minds by these desires, "they believe the abodes of the celestial gods to be "the chief object; and they devote themselves to those "texts which treat of ceremonies and their fruits, and "entice by promises of enjoyment. Such people can "have no real confidence in the Supreme Being." Thus also do the Moonduk Opunishut and the Geeta state that, "the science by which a knowledge of God "is attained is superior to all other knowledge." Therefore it is clear, from those passages of the Ved and of the Geeta, that the words of the Ved which promise fruition, are set aside by the texts of a contrary import. Moreover, the ancient saints and holy teachers, and their commentators, and yourselves, as well as we and all others, agree that Munoo is better acquainted than any other lawgiver with the spirit of the Veds. And he, understanding the meaning of those different texts, admitting the inferiority of that which promised fruition, and following that which conveyed no promise of gratification, has directed widows to spend their lives as ascetics. He has also defined in his 12th chapter, what acts are observed merely for the sake of gratifications, and what are not. "Whatever act is performed "for the sake of gratifications in this world or the next "is called Pruburttuk, and those which are performed "according to the knowledge respecting God, are "called Niburttuk. All those who perform acts to "procure gratifications, may enjoy heaven like the "gods; and he who performs acts free from desires, "procures release from the five elements of this body; "that is, obtains absorption."

Advocate.—What you have said is indeed consistent with the Veds, with Munoo, and with the Bhuguvut Geeta. But from this I fear, that the passages of the Veds and other Shastrus, that prescribe Concremation and Postcremation as the means of attaining heavenly enjoyments, must be considered as only meant to deceive.

Opponent.—There is no deception. The object of those passages is declared. As men have various dispositions, those whose minds are enveloped in desire, passion, and cupidity, have no inclination for the disinterested worship of the Supreme Being. If they had no Shastrus of rewards, they would at once throw aside all Shastrus, and would follow their several inclinations, like elephants unguided by the hook. In order to restrain such persons from being led only by their inclinations, the Shastru prescribes various ceremonies; as Shuenjag, for one desirous of the destruction of the enemy; Pootreshti for one desiring a son; and Justishtom for one desiring gratifications in heaven, &c.; but again reprobates such as are actuated by those desires, and at the same moment expresses contempt for such gratifications. Had the Shastru not repeatedly reprobated both those actuated by desire and the fruits desired by them, all those texts might be considered as deceitful In proof of what I have advanced I cite the following text of the Opunishut: "Knowledge and "rites together offer themselves to every man. The "wise man considers which of these two is the better "and which the worse. By reflection, he becomes con-"vinced of the superiority of the former, despises rites, "and takes refuge in knowledge. And the unlearned, "for the sake of bodily gratification, has recourse to "the performance of rites." The Bhuguvut Geeta: "The Veds that treat of rites are for the sake of those "who are possessed of desire; therefore, O Urjoon! "do thou abstain from desires."

Hear also the text of the Ved reprobating the fruits of rites: "As in this world the fruits obtained from cultivation and labour perish, so in the next world "fruits derived from rites are perishable." Also the Bhuguvut Geeta: "All those who observe the rites "prescribed by the three Veds, and through those "ceremonies worship me and seek for heaven, having "become sinless from eating the remains of offerings, "ascending to heaven, and enjoying the pleasures of "the gods, after the completion of their rewards, again "return to earth. Therefore, the observers of rites for "the sake of rewards, repeatedly ascend to heaven, and "return to the world, and cannot obtain absorption."

Advocate.—Though what you have advanced from the Ved and sacred codes against the practice of Concremation and Postcremation, is not to be set aside, yet we have had the practice prescribed by Hareet and others handed down to us.

Opponent.—Such an argument is highly inconsistent with justice. It is every way improper to persuade to self-destruction, by citing passages of inadmissible authority. In the second place, it is evident from your own authorities, and the Sunkulpu recited in conformity with them, that the widow should voluntarily quit life, ascending the flaming pile of her husband. But, on the contrary, you first bind down the widow along with the corpse of her husband, and then heap over her such a quantity of wood that she cannot rise. At the time too of setting fire to the pile, you press her down with large bamboos. In what passage of Hareet or the rest do you find authority for thus binding the woman according to your practice? This then is, in fact, deliberate female murder.

Advocate.—Though Hareet and the rest do not indeed authorize this practice of binding, &c., yet were a woman after having recited the Sunkulpu not to perform Concremation, it would be sinful, and considered disgraceful by others. It is on this account that we have adopted the custom.

Opponent.—Respecting the sinfulness of such an act, that is mere talk: for in the same codes it is laid down, that the performance of a penance will obliterate the sin of quitting the pile. Or in case of inability to undergo the regular penance, absolution may be obtained by bestowing the value of a cow, or three kahuns of kowries. Therefore the sin is no cause of alarm. The disgrace in the opinion of others is also nothing: for good men regard not the blame or reproach of persons who can reprobate those who abstain from the sinful murder of women. And do you not consider how great is the sin to kill a woman; therein forsaking the fear of God, the fear of conscience, and the fear of the Shastrus, merely from a dread of the reproach of those who delight in female murder?

Advocate.—Though tying down in this manner be not authorized by the Shastrus, yet we practise it as being a custom that has been observed throughout Hindoosthan.

Opponent.—It never was the case that the practice of fastening down widows on the pile was prevalent throughout Hindoosthan: for it is but of late years that this mode has been followed, and that only in Bengal, which is but a small part of Hindoosthan. No one besides who has the fear of God and man before him, will assert that male or female murder, theft, &c., from having been long practised, cease to be vices. If, according to your argument, custom ought to set aside the precepts of the Shastrus, the inhabitants of the forests and mountains who have been in the habits of plunder, must be considered as guiltless of sin, and it would be improper to endeavour to restrain their habits. The Shastrus, and the reasonings connected with them, enable us to discriminate right and wrong. In those Shastrus such female murder is altogether forbidden. And reason also declares, that to bind down a woman for her destruction, holding out to her the inducement of heavenly rewards, is a most sinful act.

Advocate.—This practice may be sinful or any thing else, but we will not refrain from observing it. Should it cease, people would generally apprehend that if women did not perform Concremation on the death of their husbands, they might go astray; but if they burn themselves this fear is done away. Their family and relations are freed from apprehension. And if the husband could be assured during his life that his wife would follow him on the pile, his mind would be at ease from apprehensions of her misconduct.

Opponent.—What can be done, if, merely to avoid the possible danger of disgrace, you are unmercifully resolved to commit the sin of female murder. But is there not also a danger of a woman's going astray during the life-time of her husband, particularly when he resides for a long time in a distant country? What remedy then have you got against this cause of alarm?

Advocate.—There is a great difference betwixt the case of the husband's being alive, and of his death; for while a husband is alive, whether he resides near her or at a distance, a wife is under his control; she must stand in awe of him. But after his death that authority ceases, and she of course is divested of fear.

Opponent.—The Shastrus which command that a wife should live under the control of her husband during his life, direct that on his death she shall live under the authority of her husband's family, or else under that of her parental relations; and the Shastrus have authorized the ruler of the country to maintain the observance of this law. Therefore, the possibility of a woman's going astray cannot be more guarded against during the husband's life than it is after his death. For you daily see, that even while the husband is alive, he gives up his authority, and the wife separates from him. Control alone cannot restrain from evil thoughts, words, and actions; but the suggestions of wisdom and the fear of God may cause both man and woman to abstain from sin. Both the Shastrus and experience show this.

Advocate.—You have repeatedly asserted, that from want of feeling we promote female destruction. This is incorrect, for it is declared in our Ved and codes of law, that mercy is the root of virtue, and from our practice of hospitality, &c. our compassionate dispositions are well known.

Opponent.—That in other cases you shew charitable dispositions is acknowledged. But by witnessing from your youth the voluntary burning of women amongst your elder relatives, your neighbours, and the inhabitants of the surrounding villages, and by observing the indifference manifested at the time when the women are writhing under the torture of the flames, habits of insensibility are produced. For the same reason, when men or women are suffering the pains of death, you feel for them no sense of compassion. Like the worshippers of the female deities, who, witnessing from their infancy the slaughter of kids and buffaloes, feel no compassion for them in the time of their suffering death; while followers of Vishnoo are touched with strong feelings of pity.

Advocate.—What you have said I shall carefully consider.

Opponent.—It is to me a source of great satisfaction, that you are now ready to take this matter into your consideration. By forsaking prejudice and reflecting on the Shastru, what is really conformable to its precepts may be perceived, and the evils and disgrace brought on this country by the crime of female murder will cease.

A
SECOND CONFERENCE
BETWEEN
AN ADVOCATE FOR, AND AN OPPONENT OF,
THE PRACTICE OF
BURNING WIDOWS ALIVE.

CALCUTTA:
1820.

TO

THE MOST NOBLE

THE MARCHIONESS OF HASTINGS,

COUNTESS OF LOUDOUN, &c. &c.

THE following tract, being a translation of a Bengalee Essay, published some time ago, as an appeal to reason in behalf of humanity, I take the liberty to dedicate to Your Ladyship; for to whose protection can any attempt to promote a benevolent purpose be with so much propriety committed?

I have the honour to remain, with the greatest respect,

YOUR LADYSHIP'S

Most obedient servant,

THE AUTHOR.

February 26, 1820.

ON CONCREMATION;

A SECOND CONFERENCE BETWEEN AN ADVOCATE AND AN OPPONENT OF THAT PRACTICE.

Advocate.—UNDER the title of Vidhayuk, or Preceptor, I have offered an answer to your former arguments. That, no doubt, you have attentively perused. I now expect your reply.

Opponent.—I have well considered the answer that, after the lapse of nearly twelve months, you have offered. Such parts of your answer as consist merely of a repetition of passages already quoted by us, require no further observations now. But as to what you have advanced in opposition to our arguments and to the Shastrus, you will be pleased to attend to my reply. In the first place, at the bottom of your 4th page you have given a particular interpretation to the following words of Vishnoo, the lawgiver: "After the death of her husband a woman shall become an ascetic, or ascend the funeral pile," implying that either alternative is optional. To this, you say, eight objections are found in the Shastrus, therefore one of the alternatives must be preferred: that is to say, the woman who is unable to ascend the flaming pile shall live as an ascetic. This you maintain is the true interpretation; and in proof you have cited the words of the Skundu Pooran and of Ungira. I answer: In every country all persons observe this rule, that meanings are to be inferred from the words used. In this instance the text of Vishnoo is comprised in five words: 1st, Mrite, "on death," 2d, bhurturi, "of a husband;" 3d, bruhmuchuryum, "asceticism;" 4th, tudunwarohunum, "ascending his "pile;" 5th, va, "or." That is, "on the death of a "husband, *his widow should* become an ascetic, or "ascend his pile." It appears, therefore, from asceticism being mentioned first in order, that this is the most pious conduct for a widow to follow. But your interpretation, that this alternative is only left for widows who are unable to ascend the flaming pile, can by no means be deduced from the words of the text; nor have any of the expounders of the Shastrus so expressed themselves.

For instance, the author of the Metakshura, whose authority is always to be revered, and whose words you have yourself quoted as authority in p. 27, has thus decided on the subject of Concremation: "The widow "who is not desirous of final beatitude, but who wishes "only for a limited term of a small degree of future "fruition, is authorized to accompany her husband."

The Smartu Bhuttacharjyu (Rhughoo Nundun, the modern law commentator of Bengal) limited the words of Ungira, that "besides Concremation there is no "other pious course for a widow," by the authority of the foregoing text of Vishnoo; and authorized the alternative of a widow living as an ascetic, or dying with her husband; explaining the words of Ungira as conveying merely the exaggerated praise of Concremation.

Secondly. From the time that Shastrus have been

written in Sungskrit, no author or man of learning has ever asserted, as you have done, that the person who, desirous of the enjoyments of heaven, is unable to perform the rites leading to fruition, may devote himself to the attainment of final beatitude. On the contrary, the Shastrus uniformly declare that those who are unable to pursue final beatitude, may perform rites, but without desire; and persons of the basest minds, who do not desire eternal beatitude, may even perform rites for the sake of their fruits.

As Vusishthu declares: "The person who does not "exert himself to acquire that knowledge of God "which leads to final absorption, may perform ceremo-"nies without expectation of reward."

"To encourage and improve those ignorant persons, "who, looking only to pleasure, cannot distinguish be-"twixt what is God and not God, the Srooti has pro-"mised rewards."

Bhuguvud Geeta.

"If you are unable to acquire by degrees divine "knowledge, be diligent in performing works with a "view to please me, that by such works you may ac-"quire a better state. If you are unable even to per-"form rites solely for my sake, then, controlling your "senses, endeavour to perform rites without the desire "of fruition."

Therefore, to give the preference to self-immolation, or to the destruction of others, for the sake of future reward, over asceticism, which gives a prospect of eternal beatitude, is to treat with contempt the authorities of the Veds, the Vedant, and other Durshuns, as well as of the Bhuguvud Geeta and many others. As the Ved says: "Knowledge and rites both offer themselves to man; but he who is possessed of wisdom, "taking their respective natures into serious consideration, distinguishes one from the other, and chooses "faith, despising fruition; while a fool, for the sake of "advantage and enjoyment, accepts the offer of rites."

Without entirely rejecting the authority of the Geeta, the essence of all Shastrus, no one can praise rites performed for the sake of fruition, nor recommend them to others; for nearly half of the Bhuguvud Geeta is filled with the dispraise of such works, and with the praise of works performed without desire of fruition. A few of those passages have been quoted in the former conference, and a few others are here given.

"Works performed, except for the sake of God, "only entangle the soul. Therefore, O Urjoon, forsaking desire, perform works with the view to please "God."

"The person who performs works without desire of "fruition, directing his mind to God, obtains eternal "rest. And the person who is devoted to fruition, "and performs works with desire, he is indeed inextricably involved."

"Oh, Urjoon, rites performed for the sake of fruition are degraded far below works done without "desire, which lead to the acquisition of the knowledge of God. Therefore perform thou works without desire of fruition, with the view of acquiring "divine knowledge. Those who perform works for the "sake of fruition are most debased."

"It is my firm opinion, that works are to be performed, forsaking their consequences, and the prospect of their fruits."

The Geeta is not a rare work, and you are not unacquainted with it. Why then do you constantly mislead women, unacquainted with the Shastrus, to follow a debased path, by holding out to them as temptations the pleasures of futurity, in defiance of all the Shastrus, and merely to please the ignorant?

You have said, that eight objections are to be found in the Shastrus to the optional alternative deduced from the works of Vishnoo. To this I reply, First. To remove an imaginary difficulty, a violation of the obvious interpretation of words, whose meaning is direct and consistent, is altogether inadmissible. Secondly. Former commentators, finding no such objection to the interpretation given to the words of Vishnoo, as allowing the optional alternative of asceticism or concremation, have given the preference to asceticism. The author of the Metakshura, quoting this text of Vishnoo in treating of Concremation, makes no allusion to such an objection, but finally declares in favour of asceticism.

Thirdly. Even allowing an optional alternative to be liable to the eight objections, former authors have on many occasions admitted such an alternative. For example:—

Srooti. "Oblations are to be made of wheat or of "barley." But the meaning of this is not, according to your mode of interpretation, "That if it cannot be "made of barley, an offering is to be made of wheat."

"Burnt offering is to be made at sunrise or before "sunrise." In this instance your mode of explanation may be applied; but no authors have ever given such an interpretation, but all have admitted the alternative to be optional.

Here also, according to your opinion, the meaning would be, that if you cannot worship Shivu you should worship Vishnoo. But no authors have ever given such an interpretation to those words, and to give more or less worship to Shivu than to Vishnoo is quite contrary to the decision of all the Shastrus.

Fourthly.—The following text has also been quoted by you in opposition to the optional alternative in question, taken as you assert from the Skundu Pooran:—

" On the death of her husband, if by chance a woman " is unable to perform Concremation, nevertheless she " should preserve the virtue required of widows. If she " cannot preserve that virtue, she must descend to " hell." To confirm this text you have quoted the words of Ungira:

" There is no other pious course for a widow besides " Concremation;" which you have interpreted, that " for a widow there is no other course so pious."

I answer, the words of Ungira are express, that there is no other pious course for a widow than Concremation. And the Smartu commentator, having thus interpreted the text, in reconciling it with the words of Vishnoo already quoted, declares, that it conveys merely exaggerated praise of Concremation.

But you, in opposition to the true meaning of the expression and to the interpretation given by the Smartu commentator, have explained those words to suit your own argument, that there is no other course more pious than that of Concremation. Perverting thus the meaning of the Shastrus, what benefit do you propose by promoting the destruction of feeble woman, by holding up the temptation of enjoyments in a future state? This I am at a loss to understand.

If the passage you have quoted from the Skundu Pooran really exist, the mode in which the Smartu commentator has explained the words of Ungira ("there "is no other virtuous course,") must be applied to those of the Skundu Pooran, *viz.* that the text of the Skundu Pooran which contradicts Munoo, Vishnu, and others, is to be understood as merely conveying exaggerated praise; because, to exalt Concremation, which leads to future enjoyments that are treated as despicable by the Opunishuds of the Veds and Smriti, and by the Bhuguvud Geeta, above asceticism, in which the mind may be purified by the performance of works, without desire that may lead to eternal beatitude, is every way inadmissible, and in direct opposition to the opinions maintained by ancient authors and commentators.

Section II.

In the latter end of the 7th page you have admitted, that the sayings of Ungira, Vishnoo, and Hareet, on the subject of Concremation, are certainly at variance with those of Munoo; but assert, that any law given by Munoo, when contradicted by several other lawgivers, is to be considered annulled:—therefore, his authority in treating of the duties of widows is not admissible, on account of the discord existing between it and passages of Hareet, and Vishnoo, and others. With a view to establish this position you have advanced three arguments—the first of them is, that Vrihusputi says, "whatever law is contrary to the "law of Munoo, is not commendable;" in which the nominative case, "whatever law," as being used in the singular number, signifies, that in case laws, given by a single person, stand in opposition to those of Munoo, they are not worthy of reverence; but if several persons differ from Munoo in any certain point, his authority must be set aside. I reply, it has been the invariable practice of ancient and modern authors, to explain all texts of law so as to make them coincide with the law of Munoo; they in no instance declare that the authority of Munoo is to be set aside, in order to admit that of any other lawgiver. But you have, on the contrary, set aside the authority of Munoo, on the ground of inconsistence with the words of two or three other authors. In this you not only act contrary to the practice of all commentators, but moreover, in direct opposition to the authority of the Ved: for the Ved declares, "whatever Munoo lays down, that is commendable;" which text you have yourself quoted in p. 7. And as to what you have said respecting the words of Vrihusputi as being in the singular number, and therefore only applicable to a case in which Munoo is opposed by only one lawgiver, it is obvious that the word "whatever," being a general term, includes every particular case falling under it; and therefore his law must be followed, whatever number of authors there may be who lay down a different direction. And the reason of this is expressed in the former part of the verse of Vrihusputi, that "Munoo has in his work collected the "meaning of the Veds." From this it follows, that whatever law is inconsistent with the code of Munoo, which is the substance of the Ved, is really inconsistent with the Ved itself, and therefore inadmissible. Admitting the justice of your explanation of Vrihusputi's text, that the authority of any individual lawgiver, who is inconsistent with Munoo, must be set aside; but that when several authorities coincide in laying down any rule inconsistent with his law, they are to be followed; one might on the same principle give a new explanation to the following text:—

"The person who attempts to strike a Brahmun "goes to the hell called Sutnuyat, or of a hundred "punishments; and he who actually strikes a Brahmun, "goes to the hell of Suhusruyat, or a thousand punishments."

Here, also, the noun in the nominative case, and that in the accusative case also, are both in the singular number; therefore, according to your exposition, where two or three persons concur in beating a Brahmun, or where a man beats two or three Brahmuns, there is no crime committed. There are many similar instances of laws, the force of which would be entirely frustrated by your mode of interpretation.

You have argued in the second place, that the practice of Concremation is authorized by a text of the Rig Ved, and consequently the authority of Munoo is superseded by a higher authority. I reply: in the 12th line of the 9th page of your tract, you have quoted and interpreted a text of the Veds, expressing that "the "mind may be purified so as to seek a knowledge of "God from which absorption may accrue, by the performance of the daily and occasional ceremonies, "without the desire of fruition; therefore, while life "may be preserved, it ought not to be destroyed."

With this then and all similar texts, there is the most evident concord with the words of Munoo. Notwithstanding your admission to this effect, you assert that the authority of the Veds contradicts the declaration of Munoo. From the text already quoted, "that whatever Munoo has declared is to be accepted," it follows that there can be no discrepancy between Munoo and the Ved. But there is certainly an apparent inconsistency between the text quoted from the ceremonial part of the Rig Ved authorizing Concremation, and that above quoted from the spiritual parts of the Ved, to which the celebrated Munoo has given the preference; well aware that such parts of the Ved are of more authority than the passages relating to debased ceremonies. He has accordingly directed widows to live, practising austerities. The text of the Rig Ved, of course, remains of force to those ignorant wretches who are fettered with the desire of fruition, which debars them from the hope of final beatitude. This too has been acknowledged by yourself, in p. 11, l. 17, and was also fully considered in the first Conference, p. 13, line 18. You cannot but be aware too, that when there is a doubt respecting the meaning of any text of the Ved, that interpretation which has been adopted by Munoo, is followed by both ancient and modern authors. In the Bhuvishyu Pooran, Muhadev gave instructions for the performance of a penance for wilfully slaying a Brahmun; but observing that this was at variance with the words of Munoo, which declare that there is no expiation for wilfully killing a Brahmun, he does not set aside the text of Munoo founded on the Veds by his own authority, but explains the sense in which it is to be accepted. "The object of the declaration of Munoo, that there is no expiation for the "wilful murder of a Brahmun, was the more absolute "prohibition of the crime; or it may be considered as "applicable to Kshutrees, and the other tribes." The great Muhadev, then, did not venture to set aside the words of Munoo, but you have proposed to set up the texts of Hareet and Ungira as of superior authority.

Thirdly.—You have quoted, with the view of doing away with the authority of Munoo, the text of Juemini, signifying that if there be a difference of opinion respecting a subject, then the decision of the greater number must be adopted; and therefore, as the authority of Munoo, in the present instance, is at variance with several writers, it must yield to theirs. I reply; it is apparent that this text, as well as common sense, only dictates, that where those who differ in opinion are equal in point of authority, the majority ought to be followed; but if otherwise, this text is not applicable to the case. Thus the authority of the Ved, though single, cannot be set aside by the concurrent authorities of a hundred lawgivers; and in like manner the authority of Munoo, which is derived immediately from the Ved, cannot be set aside by the contradicting authorities of the others either singly or collectively. Moreover, if Ungira, Hareet, Vishnoo, and Vyas, authorized widows to choose the alternative of Concremation, or of living as ascetics; on the other hand, besides Munoo, Yugnyuvulkyu, Vusishthu, and several other lawgivers have prescribed asceticism only. Why, therefore, despising the authorities of Munoo and others, do you persist in encouraging weak women to submit to murder, by holding out to them the temptations of future pleasures in heaven?

Section III.

The quotations from the Moonduk Opunishud and the Bhuguvud Geeta, which we quoted in our first conference, to shew the light in which rites should be held, you have repeated; and have also quoted some texts of the Veds directing the performance of certain rites, such as,

" He who desires heavenly fruition shall perform the " sacrifice of a horse."—In page 17 you have given your final conclusion on the subject to this effect: " That rites are not prohibited, but that pious works " performed without desire are preferable to works " performed for the sake of fruition; and he also who " performs those works without desire, is superior to " him who performs works for the sake of fruition."—If then works without desire are acknowledged by you to be superior to works with desire of fruition, why do you persuade widows to perform works for the sake of fruition, and do not recommend to them ráther to follow asceticism, by which they may acquire eternal beatitude? And with respect to your assertion, that " rites are not prohibited," this is inconsistent with the Shastrus; for if all the texts of the Veds and lawgivers, prohibiting rites, were to be quoted, they would fill a large volume: (of these a few have been already quoted by me in pp. 5 and 6.)—There are indeed Shastrus directing the performance of rites for the sake of fruition, but these are acknowledged to be of less authority than those which prohibit such rites; as is proved by the following text from the Moonduk Opunishud: "Shastrus are of two sorts, superior "and inferior; of these the superior are those by "which the Eternal God is approached."

In the Bhuguvud Geeta Krishnu says: "Amongst "Shastrus, I am those which treat of God."

In the Sree Bhaguvut is the following text: "Ill-"minded persons, not perceiving that the object of "the Ved is to direct us to absorption, call the "superficially tempting promises of rewards their prin-"cipal fruit; but such as know the Veds thoroughly "do not hold this opinion."

The passages directing works for the sake of fruition are therefore adapted only for the most ignorant. Learned men should endeavour to withdraw all those ignorant persons from works performed with desire, but should never, for the sake of profit, attempt to drown them in the abyss of passion. Rughoo Nundun quotes and adopts the following words: "Learned men should not persuade the ignorant to "perform rites for the sake of fruition; for it is written "in the Pooran, that he who knows the path to "eternal happiness will not direct the ignorant to "perform works with desire, as the good physician "refuses to yield to the appetite of his patient for "injurious food."

Section IV.

In p. 17, l. 13, of your treatise, you have said, that the Shastru does not admit that widows, in giving up the use of oil, and betel, and sexual pleasures, &c. as ascetics, perform works without desire, and acquire absorption. And for this you advance two proofs: the first, that it appears that Munoo directs that a widow should continue till death as an ascetic, *aiming* to practise the incomparable rules of virtue that have been followed by such women as were devoted to only one husband. From the word *aiming*, it follows, that the duties of an ascetic, to be practised by widows, are of the nature of those performed with desire. Secondly, From the subsequent words of Munoo it appears, that those widows who live austere lives ascend to heaven like ascetics from their youth; therefore, from the words ascending to heaven, it is obvious that the austerities that may be performed by them are for reward. I reply; I am surprised at your assertion, that austerities practised by widows cannot be considered as performed without desire, and leading to absorption; for whether austerities or any other kind of act be performed with desire or without desire, must depend on the mind of the agent. Some may follow asceticism or other practices for the sake of heavenly enjoyments, while others, forsaking desire of fruition, may perform them, and at length acquire final beatitude. Therefore, if a widow practise austerities without the desire of fruition, and yet her acts are asserted to be with desire of fruition, this amounts to a setting at defiance both experience and the Shastrus, in a manner unworthy of a man of learning like yourself. As to what you have observed respecting the word *aiming* in the text of Munoo, it never can be inferred from the use of that word, that the asceticism of widows must necessarily be with desire; for with the object of final beatitude, we practise the acquisition of the knowledge of God, which no Shastru nor any of the learned has ever classed amongst works performed with desire of fruition. For no man possessed of understanding performs any movement of mind or body without an object: it is those works only, therefore, that are performed for the sake of corporeal enjoyments, either in the present or in a future state of existence, that are said to be with desire, and that are, as such, prohibited, as Munoo defines: "Whatever act is performed for the sake "of gratifications in this world or the next is called "Pruberttuk; and those which are performed ac-"cording to the knowledge of God are called Ni-"burttuk."

As to your second argument, that widows leading an ascetic life are rewarded by a mansion in heaven, I reply; that from these words it does not appear that austerities should necessarily be reckoned amongst works performed for reward; for a mansion in heaven is not granted to those alone who perform works with desire, but also to those who endeavour to acquire a knowledge of God, but come short of attaining it in this life. They must after death remain for a long time in the heaven called the Brumhulok, and again assume a human form, until they have, by perfecting themselves in divine knowledge, at length obtained absorption. The Bhuguvud Geeta says distinctly:

"A man whose devotions have been broken off by "death, having enjoyed for an immensity of years the "rewards of his virtues in the regions above, at length is "born again in some holy and respectable family." Koolook Bhuttu, the commentator on Munoo, says expressly, in his observations on the text of his author, that those ascetic widows ascend to heaven like Sunuk Balukhilyu and other devotees from their youth. By this, it is clearly shewn, that those widows ascend to heaven in the same way as those pious devotees who have already acquired final beatitude, which can only be attained by works performed without desire. And hence the austerities of widows must be reckoned amongst works without desire.

Section V.

In page 18, you have asserted that a widow who undergoes Concremation has a higher reward than she who lives as a devotee; for the husband of the woman who performs Concremation, though guilty of the murder of a Brahmun, or of ingratitude or treachery towards a friend, has his sins, by her act, expiated, and is saved from hell, and her husband's, her father's, and her mother's progenitors, are all beatified, and she herself is delivered from female form.—I reply, you have stated, in page 27, commencing at the 3d line, that works without desire are preferable to those performed for the sake of fruition; while here again you say, that Concremation is preferable to asceticism. You have, however, assigned as a reason for your new doctrine, that Concremation saves progenitors as well as the husband. I have already shewn, that such promises of reward are merely held out to the most ignorant, in order to induce them to follow some kind of religious observance, and to withdraw from evil conduct. Therefore, to prefer works performed with a desire of fruition, to works without desire, merely on the ground of such exaggerated promises, is contrary to all the Shastrus. If, in defiance of all the Shastrus, you maintain that such promises of reward are to be understood literally, and not merely as incitements, still there can be no occasion for so harsh a sacrifice, so painful to mind and body, as burning a person to death in order to save their lines of progenitors; for, by making an offering of one ripe plantain to Shivu, or a single flower of Kurubeer, either to Shivu or to Vishnoo, thirty millions of lines of progenitors may be saved.

"He, who maketh an oblation of a single ripe plan-"tain to Shivu, shall with thirty millions of races of "progenitors ascend to the heaven of Shivu."

"By presenting a single Kurubeer, white or not "white, to Vishnoo or Shivu, thirty millions of races of "progenitors are exalted to heaven."

Nor is there any want of promise of reward to those who perform works without desire. In fact, rather more abundant rewards are held out for such works than those you can quote for the opposite practice. "Those who have acquired knowledge in the pre-"scribed mode can, by mere volition, save any number "of progenitors; and all the gods offer worship to the "devotees of the Supreme Being." A volume filled with texts of this kind might be easily written. Moreover, should even the least part of any ceremony performed for reward be omitted or mistaken, the fruits are destroyed, and evil is produced. But there is no bad consequence from a failure in works performed without desire, for the completion of these, even in part, is advantageous. In proof I quote the Bhuguvud Geeta: "Works without desire, if only commenced, "are never without advantage; and if any member be "defective, evil consequences do not ensue, as in works "performed with desire. And the performance of even "a small portion of a work without desire brings "safety."

There is evidently a possibility of a failure in some portion of the rites of Concremation or Post-cremation, particularly in the mode in which you perform the ceremony contrary to the directions of the Shastrus. What connection is there betwixt that mode and the enjoyment of temporary heavenly gratifications —a mode which only subjects the widow to the consequences of a violent death!

Section VI.

Again in p. 17, l. 3, you admit it to be more commendable for a widow to attend to the acquisition of knowledge than to die by Concremation; but afterwards, in order to persuade them to the practice of Concremation, and to prevent them from pursuing the acquisition of knowledge, you observe, that women are naturally prone to pleasure, are extremely devoted to works productive of fruits, and are always subject to their passions. To persuade such persons to forsake

Concremation, in order to attempt the acquisition of knowledge, is to destroy their hopes in both ways. In support of your opinion you have quoted the Geeta: "Those ignorant persons who are devoted to works "ought not to be dissuaded from performing them."

I reply; your object in persuading women to burn themselves may now be distinctly perceived; you consider women, even of respectable classes, as prone to pleasure, and always subject to their passions; and therefore you are apprehensive lest they should lose both prospects of hope, by giving up Concremation, and attempting to acquire knowledge. For this reason you lead them to the destruction of their lives, by holding out to them the temptation of future reward. It is very certain that all mankind, whether male or female, are endowed with a mixture of passions; but by study of the Shastrus, and frequenting the society of respectable persons, those passions may be gradually subdued, and the capability of enjoying an exalted state may be attained. We ought, therefore, to endeavour to withdraw both men and women from debased sensual pleasures, and not to persuade them to die with the hope of thereby obtaining sensual enjoyments, by which, after a certain period of gratification, they are again immersed in the pollutions of the womb, and subjected to affliction. The Shastrus have directed those men or women, who seek after a knowledge of God, to hear and reflect upon his doctrine, that they may escape from the grievous pain of this world; and they have also prescribed daily and occasional rites to be performed without the hope of reward by those who do not seek after divine knowledge, in order that their minds may be purified, and prepared to receive that knowledge. We, therefore, in conformity with the Shastru, make it our endeavour to dissuade widows from desiring future base and fleeting enjoyments, and encourage them to the acquisition of that divine knowledge which leads to final beatitude. Widows, therefore, by leading an ascetic life in the performance of duties without desire, may purify their minds and acquire divine knowledge, which may procure for them final beatitude. And consequently there is no reason why they should lose both objects of future hope by forsaking Concremation.

"Oh, Urjoon, by placing their reliance on me, "women and those of the lower classes of Vueishyu "and Soodru may obtain the highest exaltation."

You, however, considering women devoted to their passions, and consequently incapable of acquiring divine knowledge, direct them to perform Concremation; and maintain that, if any amongst them should not burn with their husbands, according to your final decision from the Shastrus, they must lose the hopes that belong to both practices; because, according to your opinion, they are entirely incapable of acquiring divine knowledge, and by not adopting Concremation, they give up the prospect of future gratifications. As to your quotation from the Geeta, to show that persons devoted to works ought not to be dissuaded from the performance of them, it may be observed that this text applies only to rites offered without desire of reward, though applied by you to works performed for the sake of future enjoyment, in direct inconsistency with the authority of the Geeta. The object of this, as well as of all texts of the Geeta, is to dissuade men from works performed with desire. The Geeta and its Commentaries are both accessible to all. Let the learned decide the point.

You have quoted the following text of Vusishthu: "He who, being devoted to worldly pleasures, boasts, "saying, 'I am a knower of God,' can neither obtain "the consequences procurable from works, nor attain "final beatitude, the fruit of divine knowledge."

I admit the force of this text. For whether a man be devoted to worldly pleasures or not, if he be a boaster, either of divine knowledge or of any other acquirement, he is indeed most despicable; but I am unable to see how this text, which forbids vain-glory, is applicable to the question before us, which relates to the Concremation of widows.

Section VII.

In your 20th page, you have stated for us, that we do not object to the practice of Concremation, but to the tying down of the widow to the pile before setting it on fire. I reply; this is very incorrect, for it is a gross misrepresentation of our argument; because Concremation or Postcremation is a work performed for the sake of future reward, which the Opunishud and the Geeta, and other Shastrus, have declared to be most contemptible. Consequently, relying on those Shastrus, it has been always our object to dissuade widows from the act of Concremation or Postcremation, that they might not, for the sake of the debased enjoyment of corporeal pleasures, renounce the attainment of divine knowledge. As to the mode in which you murder widows by tying them to the pile, we do exert ourselves to prevent such deeds, for those who are witnesses to an act of murder, and neglect to do any thing towards its prevention, are accomplices in the crime.

In justification of the crime of burning widows by force, you have stated, towards the foot of the same page, that in those countries where it is the custom for widows to ascend the flaming pile, there cannot be any dispute as to the propriety of following that mode: but where that is not the mode followed, and it is the practice for those that burn the corpse to place a portion of fire contiguous to the pile, so that it may gradually make its way to the pile, and at that time the widow, according to the prescribed form, ascends the pile; in this mode also there is nothing contrary to the Shastrus. You have at the same time quoted two or three authorities to shew, that rites should be performed according to the custom of the country. I reply; female murder, murder of a Brahmun, parricide, and similar heinous crimes, cannot be reckoned amongst pious acts by alleging the custom of a country in their behalf; by such customs rather the country in which they exist is itself condemned. I shall write more at large to this purpose in the conclusion. The practice, therefore, of forcibly tying down women to the pile, and burning them to death, is inconsistent with the Shastrus, and highly sinful. It is of no consequence to affirm, that this is customary in any particular country—if it were universally practised, the murders would still be criminal. The pretence that many are united in the commission of such murder will not secure them from divine vengeance. The customs of a country or of a race may be followed in matters where no particular rules are prescribed in the Shastrus; but the wilful murder of widows, prohibited by all Shastrus, is not to be justified by the practice of a few. From the Skundu Pooran: "In those matters "in which neither the Veds nor lawgivers give either "direct sanction or prohibition, the customs of a "country or of a race may be observed." If you insist that the practice of a country or of a race, though directly contrary to the directions of the Shastrus, is still proper to be observed, and to be reckoned amongst lawful acts, I reply, that in Shivukanchee and Vishnookanchee it is the custom for the people of all classes of one of those places, whether learned or ignorant, mutually to revile the god peculiarly worshipped by the people of the other—those of Vishnookanchee despising Shivu, and of Shivukanchee in the same manner holding Vishnoo in contempt. Are the inhabitants of those places, whose custom it is thus to revile Shivu and Vishnoo, not guilty of sin? For each of those tribes may assert, in their own defence, that it is the practice of their country and race to revile the god of the other. But no learned Hindoo will pretend to say, that this excuse saves them from sin. The Rajpoots, also, in the neighbourhood of the Dooab, are accustomed to destroy their infant daughters; they also must not be considered guilty of the crime of child-murder, as they act according to the custom of their country and race. There are many instances of the same kind. No Pundits, then, would consider a heinous crime, directly contrary to the Shastrus, as righteous, by whatever length of practice it may appear to be sanctioned.

You have at first alleged, that to burn a widow after tying her down on the pile, is one of the acts of piety, and have then quoted our argument for the opposite opinion, that "the inhabitants of forests and moun-"tains are accustomed to robbery and murder: but "must these be considered as faultless, because they "follow only the custom of their country?" To this you have again replied, that respectable people are not to be guided by the example of mountaineers and foresters. But the custom of burning widows, you say, "has been sanctioned by the most exemplary Pundits "for a length of time. It is the custom, then, of re-"spectable people that is to be followed, and not that "of men of no principles." I answer; respectability, and want of respectability, depend upon the acts of men. If the people of this province, who have been constantly guilty of the wilful murder of women by tying them to the pile in which they are burnt, are to be reckoned amongst the respectable, then why should not the inhabitants of mountains and forests be also reckoned good, who perpetrate murder for the sake of their livelihood, or to propitiate their cruel deities? To shew that the custom of a country should be followed, you have quoted a text of the Ved, signifying that the example of Brahmuns well versed in the Shastrus, of good understanding, and whose practice is in conformity with reason and the Shastrus, not subject to passion, and accustomed to perform good works, should be followed. And you have also quoted the words of Vyas, signifying that the authorities of the Veds and Shastrus, as well as of reason, being various, the practice pointed out by illustrious men should be adopted. I reply; you have shewn that the example of men versed in the Shastrus, and who act in conformity with reason and the Shastrus, should be followed; but can you call those who, in defiance of the Shastrus, wilfully put women to death by tying them down to the pile on which they are burned, illustrious, acquainted with the Veds, and devoted to acts prescribed by the Shastrus and by reason? If not, their example is to be disregarded. If you can call those, who wilfully tie down women to put them to death, righteous and illustrious, then there is no instance of unrighteousness and depravity. I have already said, that when any act is neither directly authorized nor prohibited by the Shastrus, the custom of the country, or of the race, should be the rule of conduct; but in the present case, the words are express in prescribing that the widow shall enter the flaming pile. But those who, in direct defiance of the authority of the Shastrus, act the part of woman-murderers, in tying down the widow to the pile, and, subsequently applying the flame, burn her to death, can never exculpate themselves from the sin of woman-murder. As to the words you have quoted from the Skundu Pooran, signifying that the arguments of one who has no faith in Shivu and Vishnoo can have no weight in the discussion of the legality of facts, I reply, this text is applicable to those who worship images. Those who worship forms under any name, and have no faith in Shivu and Vishnoo, their worship is vain, and their words to be disregarded. In the same way the words of the Koolarnuv: "He whose mouth does not "give out the smell of wine and flesh, should perform "a penance and be avoided, and is as an inferior ani- "mal. This is undoubted." These words are applicable only to those who follow the Tuntrus; and if all such texts are considered otherwise applicable than in relation to the sects to whom they are directed, there is no possibility of reconciling the variances betwixt the different Shastrus. The Shastru, treating of God, contains the following words: "Acts and rites that origi- "nate in movements of the hands, and other members "of the body, being perishable, cannot effect beatitude "that is eternal."

"Those that worship forms under appellations, con- "tinue subject to form and appellation; for no perish- "able means can effect the acquisition of an imperish- "able end."

"That man who considers the Being that is infinite, "incomprehensible, pure, extending as far as space, "and time, and vacuity, to be finite, perceptible by "the senses, limited by time and place, subject to pas- "sion and anger, what crime is such a robber of Divine "Majesty not guilty of?" That is, he is guilty of those sins which are considered as the most heinous, as well as of those that are considered ordinary sins. Therefore the words of so sinful a person can have no weight in the discussion of the legality of rites.

Section VIII.

You have stated in p. 2, that in the same manner as when part of a village or of a piece of cloth has been burnt, the village or piece of cloth is said to be burnt, so if a portion of the pile is inflamed, the whole pile may be said to be flaming. Therefore, it may with propriety be affirmed, that widows do in this country ascend the flaming pile.

I reply; you may afford gratification to those who take delight in woman-murder by such a quibble, but how can you avoid divine punishment by thus playing upon words?—for we find in the text of Hareet and of Vishnoo, the phrase "pruvivesh hootasunum," which means *entering into flames*, and the term "Sumarohed-"dhootasunum," signifying *ascending the flames*. You have interpreted these directions in this way;—that, at a considerable distance from the pile, fire may be placed, and a piece of grass or rope may connect the fire with the pile; and that thus, by ascending the pile, which has not been in the smallest degree affected by the fire, the widow may fulfil the direction of ascending and entering the flaming pile. But I beg to remark, that both in the vulgar dialect and in Sungskrit, the word "Pruvesh" expresses only the introgression of one substance into another; as for example, "Grihu pruvesh "koriachhilam," *I entered the house*; the word entered cannot be used unless I actually passed into the house. If a long bamboo be attached to the house and a rope be fastened to that bamboo, no one can in any language say, that in merely touching that rope or bamboo he has entered that house. If a single billet of wood belonging to the pile were indeed inflamed, then you might say, according to your quibble regarding the burning of the cloth and of the village, that the pile was inflamed, and the flaming pile entered; but even this is by no means the case, in the mode in which your pile is used. Unless, however, the pile is so completely in fire that the flames may surround the whole of her body, the woman cannot be said to enter into flame. You must then, before you can justify your murder of helpless women, prepare a new dictionary; but there is no great probability of its interpretations being adopted by men of knowledge.

Towards the end of the 28th page you assert, that those who tie down the woman to the pile according to the custom of the country, are not guilty of violation of the Shastrus: for it is to be understood from the words of Hareet before quoted, that until her body be burnt, the widow cannot be delivered from female form, which implies that her body ought to be completely consumed; and that it is on this account that those who burn her make her fast to the pile, lest by accident any part of the dead body should fall out of the pile, and fail of being consumed, and in that case the burning be incomplete. This practice of tying down, therefore, is also conformable to the Shastru; and those who, in burning the woman, make her fast to the pile, are not therein guilty of any sin, but rather perform a pious act. In support of this assertion you have quoted the words of Apustumbu, signifying that he who performs an act prescribed by the Shastrus, or he who persuades or permits another to perform a prescribed act, ascends to heaven; and he who commits an act forbidden by the Shastru, or who persuades or permits another to perform a prohibited action, sinks to hell.

I reply; you mean to say, that it is not in order to avoid the danger of the widow's flying from the pile from fear of the flames, or from pain, that she is made fast—but merely, lest any fragments of the body should fall from the pile unburnt, that she is tied down to the pile while alive. I ask, is it with an iron chain that the woman is made fast, or with a common rope? For by securing the body by means of iron, the danger of portions of it being scattered from the pile may undoubtedly be avoided. But if, on the contrary, the body is bound with a common rope, the rope will be consumed before life has altogether quitted the body, and the rope, when so burned, can be of no use in retaining within the pile the members of the body. So far have Pundits been infatuated, in attempting to give the appearance of propriety to improper actions, that they have even attempted to make people believe, that a rope may remain unconsumed amidst a flaming fire, and prevent the members of a body from being dispersed from the pile. Men of sense may now judge of the truth of the reason to which you ascribe the practice of tying down widows. All people in the world are not blind, and those who will go and behold the mode in which you tie down women to the pile, will readily perceive the truth or falsehood of the motives you assign for the practice. A little reflection ought to have convinced you of the light in which such an argument must be viewed, even by those of your friends who have the smallest regard for truth. As for the text you have quoted from Apustumbu, it might have, with more propriety, been cited by us, because it is established by that passage, that those who commit, persuade to, or permit an improper action, descend to hell; for those that are guilty of wilful woman-murder, by tying women down with ropes, and burning them to death, a practice unauthorized by the Shastrus, and considered as most heinous, and those who persuade or permit others to do so, are certainly obnoxious to the denunciation of Apustumbu. The pretext of custom of the country, or of the object of preventing portions of the body from being scattered, will not exculpate them.

You have written, in page 29, that those who, by the permission of the widow, increase the flames by throwing wood or straw on the pile, are meritorious: for he who without reward assists another in a pious act, is to be esteemed most meritorious. In confirmation, you have quoted an anecdote of the Mutshyu Pooran, that a goldsmith, by affording his gratuitous assistance in a pious act, obtained a great reward. To this I have already replied: for if those who voluntarily commit woman-murder, by tying down a widow to the pile, and holding her down with bamboos to be burnt to death, are to be reckoned as performers of a pious act, those who assist them in so doing must be esteemed meritorious: but if this be a most heinous and debased crime, the promoters of it must certainly reap the fruits of woman-murder.

In your concluding paragraph you have quoted three texts, to prove the continual observance of this practice during all ages. The first recounting, that a dove entered into the flaming pile of her deceased husband. The second, that when Dhriturashtru was burning in the flames of his hermitage, his wife, Gandharee, threw herself into the fire. The wives of Busoodev (the father of Krishnu), of Buluram, of Prudyoomnu, and of others, entered the flaming piles of their respective husbands. These three instances occurred, as narrated by the Pooran writers, within intervals of a few years towards the close of the Dwapur Yoog. You ought then to have quoted other instances, to shew the continual observance of this practice throughout all ages. Let that be as it may, you yourself cannot fail to know, that in former ages there were, as in later times, some who devoted themselves to the attainment of final beatitude, and others to the acquisition of future pleasure. Some too were virtuous, and some sinful; some believers, some sceptics. Amongst those, both men and women, who performed rites for reward, after enjoying pleasures in heaven, have again fallen to earth. Those Shastrus themselves declare this fact; but in the Shastrus that teach the path to final beatitude, the performance of rites for the sake of reward is positively forbidden. According to these Shastrus, numberless women, in all ages, who were desirous of final beatitude, by living as ascetics, attained their object. Evidence of this is to be found in the Muhabharut and other works: "The widows of the heroic *Kooroos*, who fell valiantly with their faces to the foe, and were translated "to the heaven of Bruhmá, performed only the prescribed ceremonies with water," and did not burn themselves on the piles of their husbands. I have moreover to request your attention to the fact, that in the three instances you have quoted, the very words "entered into fire" are used. In those three cases, then, it appears that the widows actually entered the flames, and therefore, whatever widow in the present time does not enter the fire, but is burnt to death by others tying her down to the pile, has not performed the ceremony according to the ancient practice you have instanced; and from rites so performed she cannot even be entitled to the temporary enjoyment of heavenly pleasures; and those who tie her down, and, pressing on her with bamboos, kill her, must, according to all Shastrus, be considered guilty of the heinous crime of woman-murder.

Section IX.

Advocate.—I alluded, in p. 18, l. 18, to the real reason for our anxiety to persuade widows to follow their husbands, and for our endeavours to burn them, pressed down with ropes: *viz.* that women are by nature of inferior understanding, without resolution, unworthy of trust, subject to passions, and void of virtuous knowledge; they, according to the precepts of the Shastru, are not allowed to marry again after the demise of their husbands, and consequently despair at once of all worldly pleasure: hence it is evident, that death to these unfortunate widows is preferable to existence; for the great difficulty which a widow may experience by living a purely ascetic life, as prescribed by the Shastrus, is obvious; therefore, if she do not perform Concremation, it is probable that she may be guilty of such acts as may bring disgrace upon her paternal and maternal relations, and those that may be connected with her husband. Under these circumstances, we instruct them from their early life in the idea of Concremation, holding out to them heavenly enjoyments in company with their husbands, as well as the beatitude of their relations, both by birth and marriage, and their reputation in this world. From this many of them, on the death of their husbands, become desirous of accompanying them; but to remove every chance of their trying to escape from the blazing fire, in burning them we first tie them down to the pile.

Opponent.—The reason you have now assigned for burning widows alive is indeed your true motive, as we are well aware; but the faults which you have imputed to women are not planted in their constitution by nature: it would be, therefore, grossly criminal to condemn that sex to death merely from precaution. By ascribing to them all sorts of improper conduct, you have indeed successfully persuaded the Hindoo community to look down upon them as contemptible and mischievous creatures, whence they have been subjected to constant miseries. I have, therefore, to offer a few remarks on this head.

Women are in general inferior to men in bodily strength and energy; consequently the male part of the community, taking advantage of their corporeal weakness, have denied to them those excellent merits that they are entitled to by nature, and afterwards they are apt to say that women are naturally incapable of acquiring those merits. But if we give the subject consideration, we may easily ascertain whether or not your accusation against them is consistent with justice. As to their inferiority in point of understanding, when did you ever afford them a fair opportunity of exhibiting their natural capacity? How then can you accuse them of want of understanding? If, after instruction in knowledge and wisdom, a person cannot comprehend or retain what has been taught him, we may consider him as deficient; but as you keep women generally void of education and acquirements, you cannot, therefore, in justice pronounce on their inferiority. On the contrary, Leelavutee, Bhanoomutee (the wife of the prince of Kurnat), and that of Kalidas, are celebrated for their thorough knowledge of all the Shastrus: moreover in the Vrihudarunyuk Opunishud of the Ujoor Ved it is clearly stated, that Yagnuvulkyu imparted divine knowledge of the most difficult nature to his wife Muitreyee, who was able to follow and completely attain it!

Secondly. You charge them with want of resolution, at which I feel exceedingly surprised: for we constantly perceive, in a country where the name of death makes the male shudder, that the female, from her firmness of mind, offers to burn with the corpse of her deceased husband; and yet you accuse those women of deficiency in point of resolution.

Thirdly. With regard to their trustworthiness, let us look minutely into the conduct of both sexes, and we may be enabled to ascertain which of them is the most frequently guilty of betraying friends If we enumerate such women in each village or town as have been deceived by men, and such men as have been betrayed by women, I presume that the number of the deceived women would be found ten times greater than that of the betrayed men. Men are, in general, able to read and write, and manage public affairs, by which means they easily promulgate such faults as women occasionally commit, but never consider as criminal the misconduct of men towards women. One fault they have, it must be acknowledged; which is, by considering others equally void of duplicity as themselves, to give their confidence too readily, from which they suffer much misery, even so far that some of them are misled to suffer themselves to be burnt to death.

In the fourth place, with respect to their subjection to the passions, this may be judged of by the custom of marriage as to the respective sexes; for one man may marry two or three, sometimes even ten wives and upwards; while a woman, who marries but one husband, desires at his death to follow him, forsaking all worldly enjoyments, or to remain leading the austere life of an ascetic.

Fifthly. The accusation of their want of virtuous knowledge is an injustice. Observe what pain, what slighting, what contempt, and what afflictions their virtue enables them to support! How many Kooleen Brahmins are there who marry ten or fifteen wives for the sake of money, that never see the greater number of them after the day of marriage, and visit others only three or four times in the course of their life. Still amongst those women, most, even without seeing or receiving any support from their husbands, living dependent on their fathers or brothers, and suffering much distress, continue to preserve their virtue; and when Brahmans, or those of other tribes, bring their wives to live with them, what misery do the women not suffer? At marriage the wife is recognized as half of her husband, but in after-conduct they are treated worse than inferior animals. For the woman is employed to do the work of a slave in the house, such as, in her turn, to clean the place very early in the morning, whether cold or wet, to scour the dishes, to wash the floor, to cook night and day, to prepare and serve food for her husband, father and mother-in-law, sisters-in-law, brothers-in law, and friends and connections! (for amongst Hindoos more than in other tribes relations long reside together, and on this account quarrels are more common amongst brothers respecting their worldly affairs.) If in the preparation or serving up of the victuals they commit the smallest fault, what insult do they not receive from their husband, their mother-in-law, and the younger brothers of their husband! After all the male part of the family have satisfied themselves, the women content themselves with what may be left, whether sufficient in quantity or not. Where Brahmuns or Kayustus are not wealthy, their women are obliged to attend to their cows, and to prepare the cow-dung for firing. In the afternoon they fetch water from the river or tank; and at night perform the office of menial servants in making the beds. In case of any fault or omission in the performance of those labours, they receive injurious treatment. Should the husband acquire wealth, he indulges in criminal amours to her perfect knowledge, and almost under her eyes, and does not see her perhaps once a month. As long as the husband is poor, she suffers every kind of trouble, and when he becomes rich she is altogether heart-broken. All this pain and affliction their virtue alone enables them to support.

Where a husband takes two or three wives to live with him, they are subjected to mental miseries and constant quarrels. Even this distressed situation they virtuously endure. Sometimes it happens that the husband, from a preference for one of his wives, behaves cruelly to another. Amongst the lower classes, and those even of the better class who have not associated with good company, the wife, on the slightest fault, or even on bare suspicion of her misconduct, is chastised as a thief. Respect to virtue and their reputation generally makes them forgive even this treatment. If, unable to bear such cruel usage, a wife leaves her husband's house to live separately from him, then the influence of the husband with the magisterial authority is generally sufficient to place her again in his hands; when, in revenge for her quitting him, he seizes every pretext to torment her in various ways, and sometimes even puts her privately to death. These are facts occurring every day, and not to be denied. What I lament is, that, seeing the women thus dependent and exposed to every misery, you feel for them no compassion, that might exempt them from being tied down and burnt to death.

ABSTRACT

OF THE

ARGUMENTS

REGARDING

THE BURNING OF WIDOWS,

CONSIDERED AS A RELIGIOUS RITE.

CALCUTTA:
1830.

ABSTRACT

OF

THE ARGUMENTS, &c.

SEVERAL Essays, Tracts, and Letters, written in defence of or against the practice of burning Hindoo widows alive, have for some years past attracted the attention of the public. The arguments therein adduced by the parties being necessarily scattered, a complete view of the question cannot be easily attained by such readers as are precluded by their immediate avocations from bestowing much labour in acquiring information on the subject. Although the practice itself has now happily ceased to exist under the Government of Bengal,* nevertheless, it seems still desirable that the substance of those publications should be condensed in a concise but comprehensive manner, so that enquirers may, with little difficulty, be able to form a just conclusion, as to the true light in which this practice is viewed in the religion of Hindoos. I have, therefore, made an attempt to accomplish this object, hoping that the plan pursued may be found to answer this end.

* The administration to which this distinguished merit is due, consisted of Lord W. C. Bentinck, governor general; Viscount Combermere, commander in chief; W. B. Bayley, Esq., and Sir C. T. Metcalfe, members of council.

The first point to be ascertained is, whether or not the practice of burning widows alive on the pile and with the corpse of their husbands, is imperatively enjoined by the Hindoo religion. To this question, even the staunch advocates for Concremation must reluctantly give a negative reply, and unavoidably concede the practice to the option of widows. This admission on their part is owing to two principal considerations, which it is now too late for them to feign to overlook. First, because Munoo in plain terms enjoins a widow to "*continue till death* forgiving all injuries, performing "austere duties, avoiding every sensual pleasure, and "cheerfully practising the incomparable rules of virtue "which have been followed by such women as were "devoted to one only husband;" (ch. v. ver. 158.) So Yagnuvulkyu inculcates the same doctrine: "A widow "shall live under care of her father, mother, son, bro-"ther, mother-in-law, father-in-law, or uncle; since, "on the contrary, she shall be liable to reproach." (Vide Mitakshura, ch. i.) Secondly, because an attempt on the part of the advocates for Concremation to hold out the act as an incumbent duty on widows, would necessarily bring a stigma upon the character of the living widows, who have preferred a virtuous life to Concremation, as charging them with a violation of the duty said to be indispensable. These advocates, therefore, feel deterred from giving undue praise to a few widows choosing death on the pile, to the disgrace of a vast majority of that class preferring a virtuous life. And in consideration of these obvious circumstances, the celebrated Smarttu Rughoonundun, the latest commentator on Hindoo law in Bengal, found himself compelled to expound the following passage of Unggira: "there is no other course for a widow beside Concremation;" as "conveying exaggerated praise of the adoption of that course."

The second point is, that in case the alternative be admitted, that a widow may either live a virtuous life, or burn herself on the pile of her husband; it should next be determined, whether both practices are esteemed equally meritorious, or one be declared preferable to the other. To satisfy ourselves on this question, we should first refer to the Veds, whose authority is considered paramount; and we find in them a passage most pointed and decisive against Concremation, declaring that "from a desire during life, of future fruition, life ought not to be destroyed." (Vide Mitakshura, ch. i.) While the advocates of Concremation quote a passage from the Veds, of a very abstruse nature, in support of their position, which is as follows: "O fire, let these women, with bodies anointed with clarified butter, eyes coloured with collyrium and void of tears, enter thee, the parent of water,* that they may not be separated from their husbands, themselves sinless, and jewels amongst women." This passage (if genuine) does not, in the first place, enjoin widows to offer themselves as sacrifices. Secondly, no allusion whatever is made in it to voluntary death by a widow *with the corpse of her husband.* Thirdly, the phrase "these women" in the passage, literally implies women then present. Fourthly. Some commentators consider the passage as conveying an allegorical allu-

* In Sungskrit writings, water is represented as originating in fire.

sion to the constellations of the moon's path, which are invariably spoken of in Sungskrit in the feminine gender:—butter implying the milky path; collyrium meaning unoccupied space between one star and another; husbands signifying the more splendid of the heavenly bodies; and entering the fire, or, properly speaking, ascending it, indicating the rise of the constellations through the south-east horizon, considered as the abode of fire. Whatever may be the real purport of this passage, no one ever ventured to give it an interpretation as *commanding* widows to burn themselves on the pile and with the corpse of their husbands.

We next direct attention to the Smrittee, as next in authority to the Veds. Munoo, whose authority supersedes that of other lawgivers, enjoins widows to live a virtuous life, as already quoted. Yagnuvulkyu and some others have adopted the same mode of exhortation. On the other hand, Unggira recommends the practice of Concremation, saying: "That a woman "who, on the death of her husband, *ascends the burning* "*pile* with him, is exalted to heaven as equal to Uroon-"dhooti." So Vyas says, "a pigeon devoted to her "husband, after his death, *entered the flames*, and, as-"cending to heaven, she there found her husband." "She who follows her husband to another world, shall "dwell in a region of glory for so many years as there "are hairs in the human body, or thirty-five millions." Vishnoo, the saint, lays down this rule: "After the "death of her husband, a wife should live as an ascetic "or ascend his pile." Hareet and others have followed Unggira in recommending Concremation.

The above quoted passages from Unggira and others,

recommend Concremation on the part of widows, as means to obtain future carnal fruition; and, accordingly, previous to their ascent on the pile, all widows invariably and solemnly declare future fruition as their object in Concremation. But the Bhugvudgeeta, whose authority is considered the most sacred by Hindoos of all persuasions, repeatedly condemns rites performed for fruition. I here quote a few passages of that book. "All those ignorant persons who attach themselves to "the words of the Shastrus that convey promises of "fruition, consider those extravagant and alluring "passages, as leading to real happiness; and say, besides them there is no other reality. Agitated in "their minds by these desires, they believe the abodes "of the celestial gods to be the chief object, and they "devote themselves to those texts which treat of ceremonies and their fruits, and entice by promises of "enjoyment. Such people can have no real confidence "in the Supreme Being." "Observers of rites, after "the completion of their rewards, return to earth. "Therefore they, for the sake of rewards, repeatedly "ascend to heaven and return to the world, and cannot "obtain eternal bliss."

Munoo repeats the same: "Whatever act is performed for the sake of gratification in this world or "the next, is called Pruvurtuk, as leading to the temporary enjoyment of the mansions of gods; and those "which are performed according to the knowledge "respecting God are called Nivurtuk, as means to procure release from the five elements of this body; that "is, they obtain eternal bliss."

The author of the Mitakshura, a work which is considered as a standard of Hindoo Law throughout Hindoostan, referring on one hand to the authority of Munoo, Yagnuvulkyu, the Bhugvudgeeta, and similar sacred writings, and to the passages of Unggira, Hareet, and Vyas on the other hand, and after having weighed both sides of the question, declares that "the widow "who is not desirous of eternal beatitude, but who "wishes only for a perishable and small degree of "future fruition, is authorized to accompany her hus-"band." So that the Smartu Rughoonundun, the modern expounder of law in Bengal, classes Concremation among the rites holding out promises of fruition; and this author thus inculcates: "Learned men "should not endeavour to persuade the ignorant to "perform rites holding out promises of fruition." Hence Concremation, in their opinion, is the least virtuous act that a widow can perform.*

* Hindoos are persuaded to believe that Vyas, considered as an inspired writer among the ancients, composed and left behind him numerous and voluminous works under different titles, as Muha Poorans, Itihashes, Sunghitas, Smriti, &c. &c., to an extent that no man, during the ordinary course of life, could prepare. These, however, with a few exceptions, exist merely in name, and those that are genuine bear the commentaries of celebrated authors. So the Tuntrus, or works ascribed to Shivu as their author, are esteemed as consisting of innumerable millions of volumes, though only a very few, comparatively, are to be found. Debased characters among this unhappy people, taking advantage of this circumstance, have secretly composed forged works and passages, and published them as if they were genuine, with the view of introducing new doctrines, new rites, or new prescripts of secular law. Although they have frequently succeeded by these means in working on the minds of the ignorant, yet the learned have never admitted the authority of any passage or work alleged to be sacred,

unless

The third and the last point to be ascertained is, whether or not *the mode* of Concremation prescribed by Hareet and others was ever duly observed? The passages recommending Concremation, as quoted by these expounders of law, require that a widow, resolving to die after the demise of her husband, should *voluntarily ascend* and enter the flames† to destroy her existence;* allowing her, at the same time, an opportunity of retracting her resolution, should her courage fail from the alarming sight or effect of the flames, and of returning to her relatives, performing a penance for abandoning the sacrifice, or bestowing the value of a cow on a Brahmun. Hence, as *voluntarily ascending* upon and *entering into the flames,* are described as indispensably necessary for a widow in the performance of this rite, the violation of one of these provisions

unless it has been quoted or expounded by one of the acknowledged and authoritative commentators. It is now unhappily reported, that some advocates for the destruction of widows, finding their cause unsupported by the passages cited by the author of the Mitakshura, by the Smarttu Rughoonundun, or by other expounders of Hindoo law, have disgracefully adopted the trick of coining passages in the name of the Poorans or Tuntrus; conveying doctrines not only directly opposed to the decisive expositions of these celebrated teachers of law, but also evidently at variance with the purport of the genuine sacred passages which they have quoted. The passages thus forged are said to be calculated to give a preference to Concremation over virtuous life. I regret to understand that some persons belonging to the party opposing this practice, are reported to have had recourse to the same unworthy artifice, under the erroneous plea that stratagem justifies stratagem.

* Unggira. † Vyas.

renders the act mere suicide, and implicates, in the guilt of female murder, those that assist in its perpetration, even according to the above quoted authorities, which are themselves of an inferior order. But no one will venture to assert, that the provisions, prescribed in the passages adduced, have ever been observed; that is, no widow ever voluntarily *ascended* on and *entered* into the *flames* in the fulfilment of this rite. The advocates for Concremation have been consequently driven to the necessity of taking refuge in *usage*, as justifying both suicide and female murder, the most heinous of crimes.

We should not omit the present opportunity of offering up thanks to Heaven, whose protecting arm has rescued our weaker sex from cruel murder, under the cloak of religion; and our character, as a people, from the contempt and pity with which it has been regarded, on account of this custom, by all civilized nations on the surface of the globe.

BRIEF REMARKS

REGARDING

MODERN ENCROACHMENTS

ON THE

ANCIENT RIGHTS OF FEMALES,

ACCORDING TO

THE HINDOO LAW OF INHERITANCE.

CALCUTTA:
1822.

BRIEF REMARKS,

&c. &c. &c.

WITH a view to enable the public to form an idea of the state of civilization throughout the greater part of the empire of Hindoostan in ancient days,* and of

* At an early stage of civilization, when the division into casts was first introduced among the inhabitants of India, the second tribe, who were appointed to defend and rule the country, having adopted arbitrary and despotic practices, the others revolted against them; and under the personal command of the celebrated Purusooram, defeated the royalists in several battles, and put cruelly to death almost all the males of that tribe. It was at last resolved that the legislative authority should be confined to the first class who could have no share in the actual government of the state, or in managing the revenue of the country under any pretence; while the second tribe should exercise the executive authority. The consequence was, that India enjoyed peace and harmony for a great many centuries. The Brahmuns having no expectation of holding an office, or of partaking of any kind of political promotion, devoted their time to scientific pursuits and religious austerity, and lived in poverty. Freely associating with all the other tribes, they were thus able to know their sentiments and to appreciate the justness of their complaints, and thereby to lay down such rules as were required, which often induced them to rectify the abuses that were practised by the second tribe. But after the expiration of more than two thousand years, an absolute form of government came gradually again to prevail. The first class

the subsequent gradual degradation introduced into its social and political constitution by arbitrary authorities, I am induced to give as an instance the interest and care which our ancient legislators took in the promotion of the comfort of the female part of the community, and to compare the laws of female inheritance which they enacted, and which afforded that sex the opportunity of enjoyment of life, with that which moderns and our cotemporaries have gradually introduced and established, to their complete privation, directly or indirectly, of most of those objects that render life agreeable.

All the ancient lawgivers unanimously award to a mother an equal share with her son in the property left by her deceased husband, in order that she may spend

class having been induced to accept employments in political departments, became entirely dependent on the second tribe, and so unimportant in themselves, that they were obliged to explain away the laws enacted by their forefathers, and to institute new rules according to the dictates of their cotemporary princes. They were considered as merely nominal legislators, and the whole power, whether legislative or executive, was in fact exercised by the Rajpoots. This tribe exercised tyranny and oppression for a period of about a thousand years, when Moosulmans from Ghuznee and Ghore, invaded the country, and finding it divided among hundreds of petty princes, detested by their respective subjects, conquered them all successively, and introduced their own tyrannical system of government, destroying temples, universities, and all other sacred and literary establishments. At present the whole empire (with the exception of a few provinces) has been placed under the British power; and some advantages have already been derived from the prudent management of its rules, from whose general character a hope of future quiet and happiness is justly entertained. The succeeding generation will however be more adequate to pronounce on the real advantages of this government.

her remaining days independently of her children; as is evident from the following passages:

Yagnuvul Kyu. "After the death of a father, let a "mother also inherit an equal share with her sons in "the division of the property *left by their father.*"

Katyayunu. "The father being dead, the mother "should inherit an equal share with the son."

Narudu. "After the death of a husband, a mother "should receive a share equal to that of each of his "sons."

Vihsnoo the legislator. "Mothers should be re-"ceivers of shares according to the portion allowed to "the sons."

Vrihusputi. "After his (the father's) death, a mo-"ther, the parent of his sons, should be entitled to an "equal share with his sons; their step-mothers also to "equal shares; but daughters to a fourth part of the "shares of the sons."

Vyasu. "The wives of a father by whom he has no "male issue, are considered as entitled to equal shares "with his sons, and all the grand-mothers (*including the "mothers and step-mothers of the father*), are said to be "entitled as mothers."

This Mooni seems to have made this express declaration of the rights of step-mothers, omitting those of mothers, under the idea that the latter were already sufficiently established by the direct authority of preceding lawgivers.

We come to the moderns.

The author of the Dayubhagu and the writer of the Dayututwu, the modern expounders of Hindu law (whose opinions are considered by the natives of Bengal as standard authority in the division of property among heirs) have thus limited the rights allowed to widows by the above ancient legislators. When a person is willing to divide his property among his heirs during his life-time, he should entitle only those wives by whom he has no issue to an equal share with his sons; but if he omit such a division, those wives can have no claim to the property he leaves. These two modern expounders lay stress upon a passage of Yagnuvulkyu, which requires a father to allot equal shares to his wives, in case he divides his property during his life; whereby they connect the term "of a father," in the above quoted passage of Vyas, *viz.*, "the wives of a "father, &c." with the term "division" understood; that is, the wives by whom he has no son, are considered in the division made by a father, as entitled to equal shares with his sons; and that when sons may divide property among themselves after the demise of their father, they should give an equal share to their mother only, neglecting step-mothers in the division. Here the expounders did not take into their consideration any proper provision for step-mothers, who have naturally less hope of support from their step-sons than mothers can expect from their own children.

In the opinion of these expounders, even a mother of a single son should not be entitled to any share. The whole property should, in that case, devolve on the son; and in case that son should die after his succession to the property, his son or wife should inherit it. The mother in that case, should be left totally dependent on her son or on her son's wife. Besides, according to the opinion of these expounders, if more than one son should survive, they can deprive their mother of her title, by continuing to live as a joint family (which has been often the case), as the right of a mother depends, as they say, on division, which depends on the will of the sons.

Some of our cotemporaries (whose opinion is received as a verdict by Judicial Courts) have still further reduced the right of a mother to almost nothing; declaring, as I understand, that if a person die leaving a widow and a son or sons, and also one or more grandsons, whose father is not alive, the property so left is to be divided among his sons and his grandsons; his widow in this case being entitled to no share in the property; though she might have claimed an equal share, had a division taken place among those surviving sons and the father of the grandson while he was alive.* They are said to have founded their opinion on the above passage, entitling a widow to a share when property is to be divided among *sons*.

In short, a widow, according to the expositions of the law, can receive nothing when her husband has no issue by her; and in a case he dies leaving only one son by his wife, or having had more sons, one of whom happened to die leaving issue, she shall, in these cases,

* This exposition has been (I am told) set aside by the Supreme Court, in consequence of the judges having prudently applied for the opinions of other Pundits, which turned out to be at variance with those of the majority of the regular advisers of the court in points of Hindoo law.

also have no claim to the property; and again, should any one leave more than one surviving son, and they, being unwilling to allow a share to the widow, keep the property undivided, the mother can claim nothing in this instance also. But when a person dies leaving two or more sons, and all of them survive and be inclined to allot a share to their mother, her right is in this case only valid. Under these expositions, and with such limitations, both step-mothers and mothers have, in reality, been left destitute in the division of their husband's property, and the right of a widow exists in theory only among the learned, but unknown to the populace.

The consequence is, that a woman who is looked up to as the sole mistress by the rest of a family one day, on the next becomes dependent on her sons, and subject to the slights of her daughters-in-law. She is not authorized to expend the most trifling sum, or dispose of an article of the least value, without the consent of her son or daughter-in-law, who were all subject to her authority but the day before. Cruel sons often wound the feelings of their dependent mothers, deciding in favour of their own wives, when family disputes take place between their mothers and wives. Step-mothers, who often are numerous on account of polygamy being allowed in these countries, are still more shamefully neglected, in general, by their step-sons, and sometimes dreadfully treated by their sisters-in-law who have fortunately a son or sons by their husband.

It is not from religious prejudices and early impressions only, that Hindoo widows burn themselves on the piles of their deceased husbands, but also from their witnessing the distress in which widows of the same rank in life are involved, and the insults and slights to which they are daily subjected, that they become in a great measure regardless of existence after the death of their husbands: and this indifference, accompanied with the hope of future reward held out to them, leads them to the horrible act of suicide. These restraints on female inheritance encourage, in a great degree, polygamy, a frequent source of the greatest misery in native families; a grand object of Hindoos being to secure a provision for their male offspring, the law, which relieves them from the necessity of giving an equal portion to their wives, removes a principal restraint on the indulgence of their inclinations in respect to the number they marry. Some of them, especially Brahmuns of higher birth, marry ten, twenty, or thirty women,* either for some small consideration, or merely to gratify their brutal inclinations, leaving a great many of them, both during their life-time and after death, to the mercy of their own paternal relations. The evil consequences arising from such polygamy, the public may easily guess, from the nature of the fact itself, without my being reduced to the mortification of particularizing those which are known by the native public to be of daily occurrence.

* The horror of this practice is so painful to the natural feelings of man, that even Madhuv Singh, the late Rajah of Tirhoot (though a Brahmun himself), through compassion took upon himself (I am told) within the last half century, to limit Brahmuns of his estate to four wives only.

To these women there are left only three modes of conduct to pursue after the death of their husbands. 1st. To live a miserable life as entire slaves to others, without indulging any hope of support from another husband. 2dly. To walk in the paths of unrighteousness for their maintenance and independence. 3dly. To die on the funeral pile of their husbands, loaded with the applause and honour of their neighbours. It cannot pass unnoticed by those who are acquainted with the state of society in India, that the number of female suicides in the single province of Bengal, when compared with those of any other British provinces, is almost ten to one: we may safely attribute this disproportion chiefly to the greater frequency of a plurality of wives among the natives of Bengal, and to their total neglect in providing for the maintenance of their females.

This horrible polygamy among Brahmuns is directly contrary to the law given by ancient authors; for Yagnuvulkyu authorizes second marriages, while the first wife is alive, only under eight circumstances:—1st. The vice of drinking spirituous liquors. 2dly. Incurable sickness. 3dly. Deception. 4thly. Barrenness. 5thly. Extravagance. 6thly. The frequent use of offensive language. 7thly. Producing only female offspring. Or, 8thly. Manifestation of hatred towards her husband. Munoo, chap. 9, v. 80. "A wife who drinks "any spirituous liquors, who acts immorally, who "shows hatred *to her lord*, who is *incurably diseased*, "who is mischievous, who wastes his property, may at "all times be superseded by another wife." 81st. "A "barren wife may be superseded by another in the

" eighth year; she, whose children are all dead, in the " tenth; she, who brings forth *only* daughters, in the " eleventh; she, who is accustomed to speak unkindly, " without delay." 82d. " But she, who, though afflicted " with illness, is beloved and virtuous, must never be " disgraced, though she may be superseded by another " wife with her own consent."

Had a magistrate or other public officer been authorized by the rulers of the empire to receive applications for his sanction to a second marriage during the life of a first wife, and to grant his consent, only on such accusations as the foregoing being substantiated, the above law might have been rendered effectual, and the distress of the female sex in Bengal, and the number of suicides, would have been necessarily very much reduced.

According to the following ancient authorities, a daughter is entitled to one-fourth part of the portion which a son can inherit.

Vrihusputi.—" The daughters should have the fourth " part of the portion to *which the sons are entitled.*"

Vishnoo.—" The rights of unmarried daughters shall " be proportioned according to the shares allotted to " the sons."

Munoo, ch. ix. ver. 118.—" To the unmarried daughters let their brothers give portions out of their own " allotments respectively. Let each give a fourth part " of his own distinct share, and they who feel disinclined to give this shall be condemned."

Yagnuvulkyu.—" Let such brothers as are already " purified by the essential rites of life, purify, by the "performance of those rites, the brothers that are left "*by their late father* unpurified; let them also purify "the sisters by giving them a fourth part of their own "portion."

Katyayunu.—"A fourth part is declared to be the "share of unmarried daughters, and three-fourths of "the sons; if the fourth part of the property is *so* small "*as to be inadequate to defray the expenses attending their* "*marriage, the sons have an exclusive* right to the pro-"perty, *but shall defray the marriage ceremony of the* "*sisters.*" But the commentator on the Dayubhagu sets aside the right of the daughters, declaring that they are not entitled to any share in the property left by their fathers, but that the expenses attending their marriage should be defrayed by the brothers. He founds his opinion on the foregoing passage of Munoo, and that of Yagnuvulkyu, which, as he thinks, imply mere donation on the part of the brothers from their own portions, for the discharge of the expenses of marriage.

In the practice of our cotemporaries, a daughter or a sister is often a source of emolument to the Brahmuns of less respectable cast (who are most numerous in Bengal), and to the Kayusths of high cast: these, so far from spending money on the marriage of their daughters or sisters, receive frequently considerable sums, and generally bestow them in marriage on those who can pay most.* Such Brahmuns and Kayusths, I

* Rajah Krissenchundru, the great-grandfather of the present ex-rajah of Nudia, prevented this cruel practice of the sale of daughters and sisters throughout his estate.

regret to say, frequently marry their female relations to men having natural defects, or worn out by old age or disease, merely from pecuniary considerations; whereby they either bring widowhood upon them soon after marriage, or render their lives miserable. They not only degrade themselves by such cruel and unmanly conduct, but violate entirely express authorities of Munoo and all other ancient lawgivers; a few of which I here quote.

Munoo, ch. 3d, v. 51. "Let no father, who knows "the law, receive a gratuity, however small, for giving "his daughter in marriage; since the man who, "through avarice, takes a gratuity *for that purpose*, is a "seller of his offspring."

Ch. 9th, v. 98. "But even a man of the servile "class ought not to receive a gratuity when he gives "his daughter in marriage; since a father who takes a "fee *on that occasion*, tacitly sells his daughter."

V. 100. "Nor, even in former births, have we heard "the *virtuous approve* the tacit sale of a daughter for a "price, under the name of nuptial gratuity."

Kashyupu. "Those who, infatuated by avarice, "give their own daughters in marriage for the sake "of a gratuity, are the sellers of their daughters, "the images of sin, and the perpetrators of a heinous "iniquity."

Both common sense and the law of the land, designate such a practice as an actual sale of females; and the humane and liberal among Hindoos lament its existence, as well as the annihilation of female rights in respect of inheritance introduced by modern expounders. They, however, trust that the humane attention of Government will be directed to those evils which are chief sources of vice and misery, and even of suicide among women; and to this they are encouraged to look forward by what has already been done in modifying, in criminal cases, some parts of the law enacted by Mohummudan legislators, to the happy prevention of many cruel practices formerly established.

How distressing it must be to the female community, and to those who interest themselves in their behalf, to observe daily that several daughters in a rich family can prefer no claim to any portion of the property, whether real or personal, left by their deceased father, if a single brother be alive; while they (if belonging to a Kooleen family or Brahmun of higher rank) are exposed to be given in marriage to individuals who have already several wives and have no means of maintaining them.

Should a widow or a daughter wish to secure her right of maintenance, however limited, by having recourse to law, the learned Brahmuns, whether holding public situations in the courts or not, generally divide into two parties, one advocating the cause of those females, and the other that of their adversaries. Sometimes, in these or other matters respecting the law, if the object contended for be important, the whole community seems to be agitated by the exertions of the parties and of their respective friends, in claiming the verdict of the law against each other. In general, however, a consideration of difficulties attending a lawsuit, which a native woman, particularly a widow, is hardly capable of surmounting, induces her to forego her right; and if she continue virtuous, she is obliged to live in a miserable state of dependence, destitute of all the comforts of life; it too often happens, however, that she is driven by constant unhappiness to seek refuge in vice.

At the time of the decennial settlement in the year 1793, there were, among European gentlemen, so very few acquainted with Sungscrit and Hindoo law, that it would have been hardly possible to have formed a committee of European oriental scholars and learned Brahmuns, capable of deciding on points of Hindoo law. It was, therefore, highly judicious in Government, to appoint Pundits in the different Zillah Courts and Courts of Appeal, to facilitate the proceedings of Judges in regard to such subjects: but as we can now fortunately find many European gentlemen, capable of investigating legal questions, with but little assistance from learned natives, how happy would it be for the Hindoo community, both male and female, were they to enjoy the benefits of the opinion of such gentlemen, when disputes arise, particularly on matters of inheritance.

Lest any one should infer from what I have stated, that I mean to impeach, universally, the character of the great body of learned Hindoos, I declare, positively, that this is far from my intention: I only maintain, that the native community place greater confidence in the honest judgment of the generality of European gentlemen, than in that of their own countrymen. But, should the natives receive the same advantages of education that Europeans generally enjoy, and be brought up in the same notions of honour, they will I trust be found, equally with Europeans, worthy of the confidence of their countrymen, and the respect of all men.

THE END.